TRADITIONAL INDIAN COOKING

TRADITIONAL INDIAN COOKING

MRS. VIJAI MEHRA

Classic Paperbacks

Traditional Indian Cooking

© Vijay Mehra : 1998
Mrs. Vijai Mehra
ISBN No. : 81-87155-05-1

Published by :
Classic Paperbacks
M-114 Vikas Puri
New Delhi-110 018

Laser Typesetting by :
Sunrise Graphics
WZ-45 Ram Nagar
New Delhi-110 018
Tel. : 5151147

Sole Distributors:
Cambridge Book Depot
3, Regal Building, Sansad Marg,
New Delhi-110 001
Phone : 336 3395
Fax : 91-11-514 1173

I dedicate this book with love to my husband Kulyash and children Deepak and Deepti who have constantly endured with me during my early experiments with cooking and who have by their constructive criticism, inspired me to cook better and tastier food.

PREFACE

There are innumerable books on cooking in market. So, why another addition? In my earlier years after marriage I tried to read such books and indeed got many ideas. But I felt that many authors had not personally tried all the dishes included by them in their books. Similarly some authors used measures like pounds, grams, pints, quarts etc. An average housewife does not have easy access to instruments of weights and measures.

In my selection of recipes in this book I have tried to restrict myself generally to traditional tasty vegetarian dishes, rather than all the fancy dishes. I have tried to include only such dishes which I have prepared dozens of times for my family or for large get-togethers. I have tried to be brief and have used commonly understood measures and names of ingredients.

I am sure this book will be found useful by a young housewife. There is no doubt that she cannot perfect her cooking by just reading the recipes. She will have to try the recipes a few times before achieving a degree of perfection. I only wish that she and her husband are patient enough before she gains proficiency in the art of cooking. The purpose of the book will be served if the reader is able to cook tastier vegetarian food.

Mrs. Vijai Mehra

CONTENTS

CHAPTER I
SOUPS & JUICES

CHAPTER II
RICE DISHES

CHAPTER III
PARATHAS & PURIS

CHAPTER IV
GRAMS & DALS

CHAPTER V
CURRIED VEGETABLES

CHAPTER VI
DRY VEGETABLE DISHES

CHAPTER VII
CURD PREPARATIONS

CHAPTER VIII
SWEETS & SWEET DISHES

CHAPTER IX
TEA TIME SNACKS

CHAPTER X
CHUTNEYS, PICKLES & JAMS

CHAPTER - I
SOUPS AND
JUICES

VEGETABLE SOUP

Serves 4-6
Preparation Time 30 Minutes

Ingredients :

200 gm tomatoes
1 large carrot
1 large potato
1 large onion
1 cm piece ginger
3-4 leaves of spinach
Salt and pepper to taste.

2 tbsp. cream
1 tsp. maida
1 slice of bread
oil for frying

Method :

Wash all the vegetables and cut into small pieces. Boil these with 4 cups of water, maida and sugar on a medium heat till the vegetables are soft. Blend in mixi. Strain through a sieve and add salt and pepper to taste.

Cut a slice of bread into small cubes and fry in hot oil till golden brown.

Serve the soup steaming hot with a little cream and a few fried bread croutons on the top of each cup.

DAL SOUP

Serves 4-6
Preparation Time 30 Minutes

Ingredients :

1 cup moong dal   1 cm piece ginger
   (without husk)   4 cloves
1 large onion   Salt and pepper to taste.
2 large tomatoes
1 tsp. jeera
1 tbsp. oil or butter

Method :

Wash and boil dal with chopped onion, ginger, cloves and 6 cups of water on medium heat till the dal is soft. Add pieces of tomatoes and boil for another 5 minutes. Blend in mixi.

Strain through a sieve and add salt and pepper to taste.

Heat oil. Put jeera and fry for 1 minute and pour in the soup.

Serve the soup steaming hot or luke warm, as desired.

PANNA

Serves 6-8
Preparation Time 30 Minutes

Ingredients :

1 kg. raw mangoes   1 cup sugar
1 tsp. jeera
1 tsp kala namak

Method :

Roast the jeera and grind it to powder.

Peel and cut the pieces of mangoes.

Put ½ cup of water and cook in pressure cooker for 5 minutes. Let it cool down. Put sugar and blend in electric mixer for 2-3 minutes. Add 6 glasses of water. Put jeera and kala namak.

Chill and serve. It has a very cooling effect in hot summers.

RASAM

Serves 6-8
Preparation Time 30 Minutes

Ingredients :

1 cup masoor dal	1 tsp. mustard seeds
1 medium size onion	1 tsp. oil
2 large tomatoes	½ tsp. jeera
A few curry leaves	½ tsp. methi seeds
25 gm. tamarind	1 tsp. coriander seeds
Salt & pepper to taste	4 dried red chillies

Method :

Roast jeera, methi seeds, coriander seeds and chillies on a tawa and grind into powder.

Wash and boil dal with 6 cups of water on medium heat till tender. Add tomatoes and onion pieces, powdered masala, salt and pepper and boil for another 10 minutes. Mix well with a big spoon.

Soak tamarind in ½ cup of water for 15 minutes. Extract the pulp. Add this pulp to the dal mixture and bring it to boil.

Heat oil. Put mustard seeds and curry leaves into it. Pour this over the rasam and serve hot.

JAL JEERA

Serves 6-8
Preparation Time 30 Minutes

Ingredients :

50 gm. tamarind	1 tsp. jeera
2 lemons	½ tsp. chilli powder
1 tbsp. podina leaves	½ tsp. pepper powder
1 tbsp. dhania leaves	Salt to taste
4 tbsp. sugar	½ tsp. kala namak

Method :

Roast jeera on a tawa. Grind it into fine powder. Wash podina and dhania leaves and grind them into fine paste.

Soak tamarind in 2 cups of water for 15 minutes. Extract the pulp through a sieve. Put lemon juice, sugar, salt, pepper, chilli powder, jeera powder, dhania and podina paste. Add another 4-5 cups of water. Cool it and serve.

KANJI

Serves 8-10
Preparation Time 3-4 Days

Ingredients :

250 gm. carrots   1 tsp. chilli powder
1 medium sized beetroot   2 tbsp. mustard seeds
Salt to taste

Method :

Grind the mustard seeds into fine powder.
Wash and cut the carrots and beetroot into thin, long pieces. Put them in a glass jar, add salt, chilli powder, mustard powder and 10 cups of boiled warm water. Mix well. Keep it in the sun for 3-4 days stirring daily 3-4 times. It gives a cherry coloured liquid. Cool it and serve. It does not get spoiled for 10-15 days without fridge.

AAM RAS

Serves 4-6
Preparation Time 10 Minutes

Ingredients :

1 kg. ripe mangoes   ½ tray ice cubes
3 tbsp. sugar (optional)

Method :

Peel and take out the pulp of mangoes. Crush the ice. Add sugar and crushed ice to the mango pulp. Blend in electric mixer for 2-3 minutes.

Serve in tall glasses. You can add more ice if you like.

TOMATO SOUP

Serves 4-6
Preparation Time 30 Minutes

Ingredients :

250 gm tomatoes	2 tbsp. cream
1 large onion	1 slice of bread
1 cm piece ginger	oil for frying
1 tsp. maida	
1 tsp. sugar	
Salt and pepper to taste.	

Method :

Wash and cut the tomatoes into four pieces each. Chop the onion and ginger. Boil tomatoes, onion, ginger, maida & sugar in 4 cups of water on a medium heat for 15 minutes. Blend in mixi. Strain through a sieve and add salt and pepper to taste.

Cut a slice of bread into small cubes and fry in hot oil till golden brown.

Serve the soup steaming hot with a little cream and a few fried bread croutons on the top of each cup.

Chapter-II Rice Dishes

MIXED VEGETABLE PULAO

Serves 3-4
Preparation Time 20 Minutes

Ingredients :

2 cups basmati or
  any good variety
  of rice
1 cup shelled peas
1 large potato
2 large carrots
1 large onion
1 bunch coriander leaves

1 tsp. jeera
6 cloves
2 black cardamoms
2 or 3 cm piece cinnamon
Salt to taste
2 tbsp. oil

Method :

Wash and soak the rice in water for half an hour.
Cut potato, carrots and onion into small pieces.

Heat oil in a thick bottomed vessel. Put jeera,
cloves, cinnamon, cardamom and onions. When onions
are brown in colour add other vegetables and fry for 2
minutes. Now add rice, salt and 4 cups of water. Bring
it to boil. Cover the lid tightly and reduce the heat very
low. Cook till the rice is tender and the water dries up
(approximately 10 minutes).

Garnish with coriander leaves and serve hot.

PEAS PULAO

Serves 3-4
Preparation Time 20 Minutes

Ingredients :

2 cups rice
2 cups shelled peas
1 large onion
Salt to taste
2 tbsp. oil

1 tsp. jeera
6 cloves
2 green cardamoms
2 or 3 cm piece cinnamon
2 tbsp. cashewnuts
2 tbsp. kishmish

Method :

Wash and soak the rice in water for half an hour. Cut onion into thin long pieces.

Heat oil in a thick bottomed vessel. Fry the onions till golden brown. Take them out and keep aside. Now put the jeera, cloves, cinnamon, cardamoms, cashewnuts, kishmish and peas in the oil and fry for 2 minutes. Put rice, salt and 4½ cup of water. Bring it to boil and reduce the heat. Cover the lid tightly. Cook till the rice is tender and the water dries up (approx. 10 minutes).

Garnish with fried onions and serve hot.

CAULIFLOWER PULAO

Serves 3-4
Preparation Time 20 Minutes

Ingredients :

2 cups rice

1 medium sized
cauliflower

1 large onion

1 small piece ginger

1 tsp. jeera

1 tsp. pepper corn

Salt to taste

2 tbsp. oil

1 bunch of coriander
leaves

Method :

Wash and soak the rice in water for half an hour. Cut onion and ginger into small pieces and flower portion of the cauliflower into big pieces.

Heat oil in a thick bottomed vessel. Put jeera, pepper corn, ginger, onion and fry till the onions are brown. Add cauliflower and fry for 2 minutes. Put rice, salt and 4 cups of water. Bring it to boil and reduce the heat. Cover the lid tightly and cook till the rice is tender (approx. 10 minutes).

Garnish with coriander leaves and serve hot.

TOMATO PULAO

Serves 3-4
Preparation Time 30 Minutes

Ingredients :

2 cups rice
½ kg. tomatoes
2 tbsp. oil
1 tbsp. butter

1 tsp. jeera
½ tsp. chilli powder
Salt to taste

Method :

Wash and soak the rice in water for half an hour. Make pulp of the tomatoes by blending them in mixi and keep aside.

Heat oil in a thick bottomed vessel. Add jeera, then rice, chilli powder, salt and 2½ cups of water. Bring it to boil, reduce the heat, add tomato pulp and cook with tightly covered lid for about 15 minutes. Add butter and serve hot.

TRICOLOUR PULAO

Serves 3-4
Preparation Time 30 Minutes
Ingredients :

2 cups rice
½ tsp. liquid red
   colour (edible)
½ tsp. liquid green
   colour (edible)
2 tbsp. oil

6 cloves
1 tsp. jeera
2 black cardamoms
2 cm piece cinnamon
Salt to taste

Method :

Wash and soak the rice in water for half an hour. Heat oil in a thick bottomed vessel. Add jeera, cloves, cardamoms, cinnamon and fry for one minute. Now put rice, salt and 4 cups of water. Bring it to boil. Reduce the heat. Cook with tightly covered lid till the rice is ready (approx. 10 minutes).

Divide the rice into 3 equal portions. Mix red colour in one portion, green in another and leave one as it is.

Grease a round cake tin. Put red coloured rice at the bottom, then white and then green at the top. Cover it with a lid.

Boil some water in a karahi, Keep this covered tin in it for 5 minutes. Cook it for 5 minutes.

Turn up side down in a serving dish and remove the tin carefully.

PEAS AND POHA PULAO

Serves 4-6
Preparation Time 20 Minutes

Ingredients :

3 cups poha
1 cup shelled peas
1 large onion
1 large potato
2 tomatoes
2 green chillis
½ cup peanuts
2 tbsp. oil

1 tsp. mustard seeds
½ tsp. chilli powder
4 dried red chillies
1 bunch of curry leaves
2 tbsp. grated fresh
   coconut
Salt to taste

Method :

Wash the poha and keep in a big strainer for 10 minutes.

Cut vegetables into small pieces.

Heat oil in a karahi. Put mustard seed, broken red chillies and curry leaves. Then add onion, potatoes, peas and peanuts and fry for 5 minutes. Add tomato pieces, green chillis, salt and chilli powder. Now add poha and mix well.

Garnish with grated coconut and serve hot.

Traditional Indian Cooking

KHICHRI

Serves 4-6
Preparation Time 20 Minutes

Ingredients :

2 cups rice	1 tsp. jeera
1 cup moong dal	1 tsp. pepper corn
(with husk)	6 cloves
1 large onion	Salt to taste
2 tbsp. oil	Pinch of hing

Method :

Wash dal and rice together and soak in water for half an hour.

Cut onion into small pieces.

Heat oil in a thick bottomed vessel. Put jeera, hing, pepper corn, cloves and onion. Fry till onions are brown in colour. Now put dal, rice, salt and 6 cups of water. Bring it to boil. Reduce the heat. Cook with tightly covered lid until the dal and rice are tender (approx. 10 minutes).

Serve hot or warm, as desired.

SWEET ZARDA PULAO

Serves 3-4
Preparation Time 30 Minutes

Ingredients :

2 cups rice	1 tsp. jeera
10 almonds	Seeds of 2 green
2 tbsp. kishmish	cardamoms
2 tbsp. cashewnuts	A pinch of saffron or
1½ cups sugar	yellow edible colour
2 tbsp. oil	2 tbsp. butter

Method :

Wash and soak the rice in water for half an hour. Mix sugar with ½ cup of water and yellow colour (edible). Boil it. Keep this syrup at a warm place.

Heat oil in a thick bottomed vessel. Put jeera and cardamom seeds. Now put rice and 2½ cups of water. Bring it to boil. Reduce the heat add cook with covered lid till water dries up (approx. 5 minutes). Add the sugar syrup, kishmish and cashewnuts. Cook covered on low heat till the rice is tender and water dries up (approx. 10 minutes). Add butter and mix.

Decorate with almond gratings and serve hot.

DAHI RICE (COLD)

Serves 3-4
Preparation Time 30 Minutes

Ingredients :

2 cups rice	4 green chillis
2 cups milk	1 tsp. mustard seeds
2 tsp. curd	A few curry leaves
Salt to taste	1 tbsp. oil

Method :

Boil rice in enough water adding salt till the rice is cooked. Remove excess water and let it cool for 2-3 hours.

Warm the milk and add curd to it. Put this milk, curd mixture in rice and mix well. Keep for 3-4 hours in a warm place.

Heat oil. Put mustard seeds, chopped green chillies and curry leaves. Pour this on the rice and mix.

This rice can be kept for 3-4 days and is good for travelling.

DAHI RICE (FRIED)

Serves 2-3
Preparation Time 20 Minutes

Ingredients :

1 cup rice

½ cup sour curd

2 green chillis

A few curry leaves

2 tbsp. ground nuts

1 tbsp. oil

Salt to taste

½ tsp. red chilli powder

1 tsp. mustard seeds

¼ tsp. haldi

1 tbsp. grated fresh coconut

Method :

Boil the rice in 2 cups of salted water for 10 minutes on low heat and let it cool.

Heat oil. Add mustard seeds, curry leaves, chopped chillis, haldi, chilli powder and peanuts. Now pour well beaten curd over them. Mix well. Add cold rice. Cook for 2 minutes.

Garnish with coconut and serve hot.

Dahi rice can be made from left over pulao also.

Chapter-III
Parathas And
Puris

BESAN PARATHAS

Serves 4-6
Preparation Time 30 Minutes

Ingredients :

2 cups atta   2 green chillis
1 cup besan   ½ tsp. red chilli powder
1 large onion   Oil for shallow frying
1 bunch podina leaves Salt to taste

Method :

Cut onion, chillis and podina into fine pieces.

Sieve atta and besan. Add onions, chillis, podina, salt, chilli powder and 1 tbsp. oil. Mix well and knead into a soft dough adding water. Let the dough stand for 15 minutes. Knead again.

Take some dough, make a ball and roll out into round paratha with the help of a little dry atta.

Heat tawa. Cook parathas on both sides putting a little oil on both the sides till light brown in colour.

Serve hot or warm.

ALU PARATHAS

Serves 4-6

Preparation Time 30 Minutes

Ingredients :

2 cups atta
4 large potatoes
1 large onion
1 bunch of coriander
leaves
2 cm. piece ginger

½ tsp. chilli powder
½ tsp. anardana
Salt to taste
Oil for shallow frying
2 green chillis

Method :

Boil potatoes till tender. Cut onion, ginger, coriander leaves and green chillis into very fine pieces. Peel and mash the potatoes. Mix potatoes, onions, coriander leaves, green chillis, salt, anardana and chilli powder together and keep aside.

Sieve atta, add a pinch of salt and make soft dough adding water.

Take some dough, make a ball. Roll it a little smear a little oil over it. Put 1 tbsp. of potato mixture over it. Gather edges and make a ball again. Roll it out into a paratha as thin as possible with the help of dry atta.

Heat tawa. Cook parathas on both sides putting a little oil till golden brown in colour.

Serve hot or warm.

Traditional Indian Cooking

MOOLI PARATHAS

Serves 4-6
Preparation Time 30 Minutes

Ingredients :

2 cups atta
4 large white moolis
1 bunch coriander
  leaves
2 cm. piece ginger

½ tsp. ajwain
½ tsp. chilli powder
Salt to taste
Oil for shallow frying
2 green chillis

Method :

Wash and grate the moolis. Apply a little salt and keep for 5 minutes. Squeeze out all the water from it by pressing with hands. Cut ginger, coriander leaves and green chillis very fine. Add to mooli along with ajwain, salt and chilli powder. Mix well and keep aside.

Sieve the atta, add a pinch of salt and make into soft dough adding water.

Take some dough and make a ball. Roll it a little and smear a little oil over it. Put 1 tbsp. of mooli mixture in the centre and make into a ball again. Roll it out into a thin paratha with the help of dry atta..

Heat tawa. Cook parathas on both sides putting a little oil till golden brown in colour.

Serve hot or warm.

PEAS PARATHAS

Serves 4-6
Preparation Time 30 Minutes

Ingredients :

2 cups atta
1 cup shelled peas
Oil for shallow frying
2 green chillis

½ tsp. chilli powder
Salt to taste
1 bunch coriander leaves

Method :

Boil peas with a little water till soft. Chop coriander leaves and green chillis very fine. Mash peas, add green chillis and coriander leaves, salt and chilli powder. Mix well and keep aside.

Sieve flour, add a pinch of salt and make into soft dough adding water.

Take some dough and make a ball. Roll it a little and smear a little oil over it. Put 1 tbsp. of peas mixture in the centre and make it into a ball again. Roll it out into paratha as thin as possible.

Heat tawa. Cook parathas on both sides adding a little oil until golden brown in colour.

Serve hot or warm.

METHI PARATHAS

Serves 4-6
Preparation Time 30 Minutes

Ingredients :

2 cups atta
1 bunch methi leaves
1 cm. piece ginger
2 green chillis

½ tsp. red chilli powder
Salt to taste
Oil for shallow fyring

Method :

Wash and cut the methi leaves, green chillis and ginger very fine.

Sieve the atta, add methi, ginger, green chillis, salt chilli powder and 1 tbsp. oil. Mix well and knead into a soft dough adding water.

Take some dough, make a ball and roll out into round paratha.

Heat tawa. Cook parathas on both sides putting a little oil on both the sides till light brown in colour.

Serve hot or warm.

GOBI PARATHAS

Serves 4-6
Preparation Time 30 Minutes

Ingredients :

2 cups atta
1 medium size gobhi
1 large onion
1 small piece ginger
1 bunch coriander leaves

2 green chillis
½ tsp. chilli powder
Salt to taste
Oil for shallow frying

Method :

Grate the flower portion of the gobhi. Cut onion, ginger, green chillis and coriander leaves very fine. Add to gobhi along with salt and chilli powder. Mix well and keep aside.

Sieve atta, add a pinch of salt and make into soft dough adding water.

Take some dough and make a ball. Roll it a little and smear a little oil over it. Put 1 tbsp. of gobhi mixture in the centre and make a ball again. Roll it out as thin as possible.

Heat tawa. Cook parathas on both sides putting a little oil till golden brown in colour.

Serve hot or warm.

KHASTA PURIS

Serves 4-6

Preparation Time 20 Minutes

Ingredients :

2 cups atta
1 cup maida
½ tsp. ajwain
2 tbsp. oil for dough

Salt to taste
Enough oil for deep frying

Method :

Sieve maida and atta. Add 2 tbsp. oil, ajwain, salt and mix well. Make a stiff dough with water. Keep for half an hour and knead again.

Make small balls from the dough. Roll them out into thin rounds with the help of oil.

Heat oil in a karahi. Fry the puris one by one in very hot oil. They should be puffed like a balloon and should be golden brown in colour.

Serve hot or cold.

KACHORIS

Serves 4-6
Preparation Time 35 Minutes

Ingredients :

2 cups atta	½ tsp. chilli powder
1 cup maida	½ tsp. dhania powder
1 cup urd dal	A pinch of hing
(without husk)	Salt to taste
1 small piece ginger	Enough oil for
	deep frying

Method :

Wash and soak the dal overnight. Grind dal and ginger together into a coarse paste without adding any water. Add hing, chilli powder and dhania powder. Mix well. Do not add salt.

Sieve atta and maida. Add salt, 2 tbsp. oil and make a stiff dough adding water. Knead well.

Make small balls from the dough. Roll one ball at a time slightly. Put 1 tsp. of dal mixture in the centre and make into ball again. Roll it out as thin as possible with the help of oil.

Heat oil in a karahi. Fry the kachoris one by one in very hot oil till brown in colour.

Serve hot.

DAL PARATHAS

Serves 4-6
Preparation Time 40 Minutes

Ingredients :

2 cups atta
1 cup urd dhuli
    channa dal
1 large onion
2 green chillis
1 small piece ginger
1 bunch coriander leaves

½ tsp. chilli powder
½ tsp. amchur
Salt to taste
Oil for shallow frying
1 tsp. whole coriander
    seeds

Method :

Wash and soak the dal over night. Grind into a coarse paste without adding water. Chop onion, green chillis, ginger and coriander leaves very fine. Add to dal along with salt, chilli powder, coriander seeds and amchur. Mix well and keep aside.

Sieve atta add a pinch of salt and make into soft dough adding water.

Take some dough and make a ball. Roll it a little and smear a little oil over it. Put 1 tbsp. of dal mixture in the centre and make a ball again. Roll it out as thin as possible.

Heat tawa. Cook parathas on both sides adding a little oil until light brown in colour.

Serve hot.

SWEET PARATHAS

Serves 4-6
Preparation Time 20 Minutes

Ingredients :

2 cups atta   Oil for shallow frying
1 cup sugar   2 tbsp. butter
2 tbsp. chopped almonds

Method :

Sieve atta and make into soft dough adding water. Take some dough and make a ball. Roll it a little and keep aside. Make another ball from the dough and roll it also a little. Smear it with oil. Sprinkle 2 tbsp. of sugar and a few chopped almonds over it and place the other rolled piece over it. Press with hand all round and roll it out as thin as possible.

Heat tawa. Put a little oil and then put the parathas over it. Cook the parathas on low heat on both sides adding oil until brown in colour.

Serve hot with butter over the parathas.

POTATO PURIS

Serves 4-6
Preparation Time 30 Minutes

Ingredients :

2 cups atta   ½ tsp. chilli powder
1 cup maida   Salt to taste
4 large potatoes   Enough oil for deep
2 tbsp. oil for dough   frying

Method :

Boil potatoes till tender. Peel and mash well when they are hot and cool these for 10 minutes.

Sieve atta and maida. Add mashed potatoes, salt, chilli powder and oil. Make a stiff dough. Put a little water, as necessary. Knead well.

Make small balls from the dough. Roll them out one by one into thin rounds with the help of oil.

Heat oil in a karahi. Fry the puris one by one in very hot oil. They should be golden brown in colour.

Serve hot.

BHATURAS

Serves 4-6
Preparation Time 40 Minutes

Ingredients :

2 cups maida   Salt to taste
½ cup thick sour curd   Enough oil for
1 tsp. baking powder   deep frying

Method :

Sieve maida and baking powder together. Add salt and curd in it. Mix well and make a soft dough adding warm water to it. Cover it with a wet cloth and keep in a warm place for about 6 hours. Knead it well again.

Make small balls from the dough. Roll them out into not very thin rounds.

Heat oil in a karahi. Fry bhaturas one by one in very hot oil till they are light brown in colour.

Serve hot with kabuli channa.

PALAK PURIS

Serves 4-6
Preparation Time 30 Minutes

Ingredients :

2 cups atta	Salt to taste
1 cup maida	½ tsp. chilli powder
250 gm. palak leaves	Enough oil for
1½ tbsp. oil for dough	deep frying

Method :

Boil and grind the palak leaves. Mix with atta, maida, oil, salt and chilli powder. Make a soft dough by adding water. Knead it well.

Make small balls from the dough. Roll them out into thin rounds.

Heat oil in a karahi. Fry these puris one by one on high heat.

Serve hot.

Serve hot.

Chapter-IV
Grams And
Dals

SABUT URD

Serves 4-6
Preparation Time 60 Minutes

Ingredients :

1 cup urd (whole)
1 medium size onion
1 small piece ginger
½ tsp. chilli powder
Salt to taste
3 tbsp. oil or ghee

A bunch of coriander leaves
A pinch of hing
6 cloves of garlic
2 green chillis

Method :

Cut onions, ginger, garlic, green chillis and coriander leaves into small pieces.

Clean and wash the dal. Add 6 cups of water, salt, green chillis and ginger. Cook in pressure cooker for 45 minutes on a medium heat. Mash the dal a little. Add a little more water, if necessary and reboil.

Heat oil in a frying pan. Put hing, onions and garlic. When onions are light brown in colour add the chilli powder. Pour this into dal.

Garnish with coriander leaves and serve hot.

DAL MAKHNI

Serves 4-6
Preparation Time 60 Minutes

Ingredients :

1 cup urd (whole)
1 cup curd
2 tbsp. butter
2 tbsp. oil
2 tbsp. cream
½ tsp. chilli powder
2 green chillis

1 medium size onion
1 cm piece ginger
6 cloves of garlic
1 bunch of coriander
  leaves
Salt to taste
A pinch of hing

Method :

Cut the onion, ginger, garlic, green chillis and coriander leaves into small pieces.

Clean and wash the dal. Add 6 cups of water, salt, green chillis and ginger. Cook in pressure cooker for 45 minutes on a medium heat. Mash the dal a little.

Add curd and butter to the dal and cook for another 10 minutes on a low heat stirring occasionally.

Heat oil in a frying pan. Put hing, onions and garlic. When onions are light brown in colour add the chilli powder. Pour this into dal and mix well.

Garnish with coriander leaves and cream.
Serve hot.

KABULI CHANNA

Serves 4-6
Preparation Time 70 Minutes

Ingredients :

2 cups kabuli channa *whit gram*

1 large onion

1 small piece ginger

1 tsp. garam masala

¼ tsp. pepper

½ tsp. chilli powder

1 bunch of coriander leaves

2 tsp. dhania powder *coriander*

2 tsp. amchur or ground anardana

2 green chillis

1 large tomato

½ tsp. baking powder

2 tbsp. oil

Salt to taste

Method :

Clean, wash and soak the channas in water overnight.

Cut onion, ginger, garlic, green chillis and coriander leaves into small pieces. Cut tomatoes into thin rounds.

Boil channa with 6 cups of water, ginger, green chillis, salt and baking powder in a pressure cooker for 40 minutes on a medium heat. Mash the channa a little.

Heat oil in a karahi. Add dhania, amchur, chilli powder, pepper and garam masala. Add the channa and mix well. Cook for another half an hour on low heat.

Add a little water, if necessary. Channa should be of medium consistency when ready.

Garnish with coriander leaves. Decorate with tomato rings.

HORSE GRAM

Serves 4-6
Preparation Time 50 Minutes

Ingredients :

2 cups black gram	1 tsp. dhania powder
2 large onions	1 tsp. amchur
1 small piece ginger	1 tsp. garam masala
2 green chillis	½ tsp. chilli powder
1 bunch of coriander	3 tbsp. oil
leaves	Salt to taste

Method :

Clean, wash and soak channa in water overnight.

Cut onions, ginger, green chillis and coriander leaves into small pieces.

Boil channa with 6 cups of water and salt in a pressure cooker for 30 minutes on a medium heat. Take out the water, if any.

Heat oil in a karahi. Fry onions, green chillis and ginger till onions are golden brown. Add dhania, amchur, chilli powder, garam masala and channa. Mix them well. Now add the remaining water, if there is any. Cook on medium heat till the water dries up and oil appears.

Garnish with coriander leaves and serve hot.

SUKHI DAL

Serves 4-6

Preparation Time 25 Minutes

Ingredients :

- 2 cups urd or moong dal (without husk)
- 1 large onion
- 1 small piece ginger
- 1 large tomato
- 2 cardamoms
- 2 green chillis
- 5-6 cloves of garlic
- Salt to taste
- ½ tsp. chilli powder
- ½ tsp. turmeric powder
- ½ tsp. garam masala
- 1 tsp. jeera
- 5-6 cloves
- 1 bunch coriander leaves
- 2 bay leaves
- 2 tbsp. oil

Method :

Clean, wash and soak the dal in water for half an hour.

Cut onion, garlic and ginger into thin long strips and green chillis into small pieces.

Heat oil. Put jeera, crushed cardamoms, garlic, onions, bay leaves, cloves, ginger and green chillis and fry for 2 minutes. Add dal, salt, turmeric powder, chilli powder and 2 cups of water. Cook with a tight lid and on a low heat till water dries and dal is soft. Sprinkle garam masala.

Garnish with coriander leaves and decorate with tomato rings.

PINDI CHOLEY (SPICY CHICKPEAS)

Serves 4-6
Preparation Time 50 Minutes

Ingredients :

2 cups dry Kabli channa *whit gram*	1 tsp. jeera *cumin*
2 large onions	½ tsp. red chilli powder
2 large tomatoes	½ tsp. garam masala
7-8 green chillis	2-3 bay leaves
4 tbsp. anardana *pomegranate seeds*	2 black cardamoms
4 tbsp. oil	2 cm. piece cinnamon
1 tbsp. coriander leaves	½ tsp. pepper powder
2 cm. piece ginger	2 tbsp. dhania powder *coriander*

Method :

Wash and soak channas for 6-7 hours. Cook in pressure cooker with four cups of water and salt for half an hour or more till soft. Put jeera, bay leaves, cardamoms and cinnamon also while boiling.

Roast anardana and grind it dry.

Chop onions, green chillis and ginger in long thin pieces.

Heat oil. Fry dhania powder till dark brown in colour. Add onions and fry till golden brown. Sprinkle some water and cook for 5 minutes, stirring occasionally. Add green chillis, one chopped tomato, pepper powder, anardana, salt and channas.

Cook the channas, stirring continuously till well

blended and leaves oil. Add garam masala and keep covered for 5 minutes. Add pieces of the 2nd tomato.

Transfer to a serving dish.

Garnish with coriander leaves, ginger slices and onion rings.

Serve with nan, tandoori roti, puris or bhaturas.

RAJMA

Serves 4-6
Preparation Time 60 Minutes

Ingredients :

2 cups rajma *Red beans*
3 large onions
2 green chillis
1 small piece ginger
½ pod garlic
Salt to taste

½ tsp. chilli powder
½ tsp. garam masala
½ tsp. turmeric powder
2 tbsp. oil
3 large tomatoes
1 bunch coriander leaves

Method :

Clean, wash and soak the rajma overnight.

Grind the onions, ginger, garlic and green chillis into fine paste.

Boil the rajma with salt and 6 cups of water in a pressure cooker for 30 minutes. Mash the rajma a little.

Heat oil. Fry the ground masala till brown in colour. Add the chopped tomatoes, turmeric and chilli powder. Fry for 5 minutes. Now add the rajma and 1 cup of water. Cook on low heat for 15 minutes.

Garnish with coriander leaves and serve hot with boiled rice.

SAMBER

Serves 6-8
Preparation Time 50 Minutes

Ingredients :

2 cups arhar dal	1 tsp. mustard seeds
8 small onions	½ tsp. chilli powder
25 gm. tamarind	1 tsp. dhania powder
6 red chillis (dried)	2 tsp. samber powder
1 bunch curry leaves	½ tsp. turmeric powder
1 tbsp. oil	A pinch of hing
Salt to taste	

Method :

Peel and cut onions into halves.

Soak tamarind in half a cup of water and extract pulp through a sieve.

Clean and wash the dal. Cook dal with salt, chilli powder, turmeric and 6 cups of water in a pressure cooker for 10 minutes. Mash the dal nicely.

Heat oil. Put hing, mustard seeds, dhania powder, chillis, curry leaves and onions. Fry for 2 minutes. Put juice of tamarind and samber powder. Pour the dal into this mixture and cook for 10 minutes on a low heat.

Serve hot with boiled rice.

Traditional Indian Cooking

CHANNA DAL WITH LAUKI

Serves 4-6
Preparation Time 30 Minutes

Ingredients :

1 cup channa dal	½ tsp. turmeric powder
250 gm. lauki *Harrow*	½ tsp. chilli powder
1 large onion	½ tsp. jeera
1 large tomato	½ tsp. mustard seeds
2 green chillis	Salt to taste
2 tbsp. grated fresh coconut	2 tbsp. oil

Method :

Scrape and cut the lauki into big pieces. Cut onions and green chillis into small pieces.

Clean and wash the dal. Add salt, chilli powder, turmeric powder and 2 cups of water to the dal. Cook on medium heat till the dal is half cooked. Add lauki and cook till dal is soft.

Heat oil in a karahi. Put jeera, mustard seeds, green chillis and onions. Fry till the onions are brown. Add the tomato pieces and fry for another 2 minutes. Now add dal and lauki and cook till the water dries up.

Garnish with grated coconut. Serve hot.

Chapter-V
Curried
Vegetables

MATTAR PANEER

Serves 4-6
Preparation Time 30 Minutes

Ingredients :

4 cups milk
1 cup shelled peas
2 large onions
2 large tomatoes
1 piece ginger
6 cloves of garlic
1 lemon

½ tsp. chilli powder
¼ tsp. turmeric powder
½ garam masala
Salt to taste
1 tbsp. oil
2 green chillis
1 bunch of coriander leaves

Method :

To make paneer boil the milk and add juice of a lemon. When it curdles, strain through a muslin cloth and press under a heavy pan for 10 minutes. Cut into square pieces and keep aside.

Grind onion, garlic, ginger and green chillis into a fine paste.

Heat oil. Put ground masala and fry till golden brown. Add chopped tomatoes, salt, turmeric and chilli powder. Fry for 5 minutes adding a little water, if necessary. Add the peas and 2 cups of water. Bring it to boil and reduce the heat. Cook covered until the peas are soft. Now add the paneer and garam masala. Let it simmer for 5 minutes.

Garnish with coriander leaves.

ALU MATTAR

Serves 4-6
Preparation Time 20 Minutes

Ingredients :

4 potatoes	2 large tomatoes
(medium size)	½ tsp. chilli powder
1 cup shelled peas	¼ tsp. turmeric powder
1 large onion	(½ tsp. garam masala)
1 piece ginger	Salt to taste
6 cloves of garlic	2 tbsp. oil
2 green chillis	

Method :

Grind the onions, ginger, garlic and green chillis into a fine paste.

Peel and cut the potatoes into four pieces each.

Heat oil. Fry the ground masala till brown. Add pieces of tomatoes, salt, chilli powder and turmeric powder. Fry it on low heat till the masala releases oil. Now add the potatoes and peas. Fry for two minutes and add two cups of water. Bring it to boil and reduce the heat. Cook covered till the potatoes and peas are tender. Add garam masala and garnish with coriander leaves.

ALU DUM

Serves 4-6
Preparation Time 40 Minutes

Ingredients :

12 small potatoes	4 tbsp. oil
3 large onions	½ tsp. chilli powder
1 small piece ginger	½ tsp. garam masala
6 cloves of garlic	1 tsp. dhania powder
2 large tomatoes	¼ tsp. turmeric powder
1 cup of thick curd	2 green chillis
Salt to taste	2 tbsp. coriander leaves

Method :

Grind the onions, garlic, ginger and green chillis into a fine paste.

Peel, wash and prick the potatoes with a fork.

Heat 2 tbsp. oil and fry the potatoes till golden brown.

Heat remaining oil. Brown the ground masala. Add chopped tomatoes, dhania, salt, turmeric and chillis. Fry it for some time until it leaves oil. Put fried potatoes and one cup of water. Bring it to boil and reduce the heat. Cook till the potatoes are tender. Add well beaten curd and garam masala. Let it simmer for five to ten minutes. Gravy should be very thick.

Garnish with coriander leaves and serve.

STUFFED TOMATOES WITH GRAVY

Serves 4-6
Preparation Time 40 Minutes

Ingredients :

8 ripe hard tomatoes (medium size)	¼ cup shelled peas
4 potatoes (medium size)	1 cup thick curd
2 large onions	2 tbsp. oil
2 green chillis	½ tsp. chilli powder
1 piece ginger	½ tsp. garam masala
6 cloves of garlic	¼ tsp. turmeric powder
	Salt to taste

Method :

Boil the potatoes till tender. Peel and mash them. Boil peas with a little water till tender. Mix potatoes and peas. Add a little salt and chilli powder.

Cut out a slice from the top of each tomato. Scoop out the pulp. Keep upside down for 5 minutes. Fill all the tomatoes with potatoes and peas mixture.

Grind the onions, ginger, garlic and green chillis to a fine paste.

Heat oil. Brown the ground masala. Add the pulp of the tomatoes, salt, chillis and turmeric. Fry it for 5 minutes. Add well beaten curd and let it simmer on low heat for 10 minutes. Add garam masala. The gravy is ready.

Arrange stuffed tomatoes in a shallow serving dish. Pour hot gravy over these and serve immediately.

KARELA CURRY

Serves 4-6
Preparation Time 30 Minutes

Ingredients :

250 gm. karelas   Salt to taste
(bitter gourd)   ½ tsp. dhania powder
2 large onions   ½ tsp. chilli powder
2 large tomatoes   ¼ tsp. turmeric powder
½ cup sour curd   ½ tsp. garam masala
Oil for deep frying

Method :

Scrape the karelas. Slit them on one side and apply
salt all over them. Keep them for 2-3 hours. Wash them
thoroughly. Squeeze to remove the water.

Grind the onions into a fine paste.

Heat oil in a karahi and fry the karelas till golden
brown.

Heat 1 tbsp. oil. Brown the onion paste. Add salt,
chillis, turmeric, dhania and pieces of tomatoes. Fry till
the masala releases oil. Now add the well beaten curd
and fried karelas. Let it simmer for 5-10 minutes till the
gravy thickens.

PUMPKIN CURRY

Serves 4-6
Preparation Time 20 Minutes

Ingredients :

250 gm. pumpkin
1 cup thick curd
Oil for frying
Salt to taste

½ tsp. mustard seeds
½ tsp. chilli powder
¼ tsp. turmeric powder
½ tsp. dhania powder
½ tsp. jeera

Method :

Peel and cut the pumpkin into square pieces.

Heat oil and deep fry the pumpkin pieces till golden brown.

Heat 1 tbsp. oil. Put mustard seeds and jeera. Add well beaten curd and other masalas. Add pumpkin pieces also and let it simmer on a low heat till the pumpkin is tender and gravy thickens.

SARSON KA SAAG

Serves 4-6
Preparation Time 50 Minutes

Ingredients :

500 gm. sarson	2 tbsp. butter
250 gm. spinach	Salt to taste
2 cm. piece ginger	2 green chillis
1 small onion	½ tsp. chilli powder
2 tbsp. oil	Pinch of hing
6-7 cloves of garlic	

Method :

Cut the sarson and spinach very fine. Wash thoroughly and cook in the pressure cooker with one cup of water for about 45 minutes. Add salt, chilli powder, ginger and green chillis. Grind the sag into a fine paste.

Heat oil. Put hing, garlic and finely chopped onion. Fry till light brown in colour. Add sag and let it simmer for 5 to 10 minutes on low heat.

Serve with butter at the top.

KHOYA MATTAR

Serves 4-6
Preparation Time 40 Minutes

Ingredients :

2 cups shelled peas	200 gm. khoya
2 large onions	½ tsp. turmeric powder
2 large tomatoes	¼ tsp. chilli powder
2 tbsp. cashew nuts	1 tsp. dhania powder
2 tbsp. kishmish	Salt to taste
½ cup makhanas	3 tbsp. oil
½ tsp. garam masala	2 tbsp. cream or malai

Method :

Boil the peas with a pinch of salt and a little water till soft.

Cut onion and cashew nuts into small pieces.

Heat oil. Fry the makhanas and cashew nuts till golden brown. Drain them and keep aside. Now fry the onions in the remaining oil till golden brown. Add dhania powder, salt, turmeric powder, chilli powder and chopped tomatoes. Fry for 5 minutes. Add mattar, mashed khoya, kishmish, makhanas and galved cashewnuts. Fry for 2 minutes. Add half a cup of water and let it simmer on low heat for 10 minutes. Mix malai or cream.

Sprinkle garam masala and decorate with remaining cashewuts.

NARGISI KOFTAS

Serves 4-6

Preparation Time 40 Minutes

Ingredients :

4 large potatoes	2 large tomatoes
2 tbsp. shelled peas	½ cup thick curd
2 tbsp. besan	A pinch of edible
Paneer made from	yellow colour
two cups of milk	½ tsp. chilli powder
2 large onions	½ tsp. garam masala
1 cm. piece ginger	¼ tsp. turmeric powder
Oil for frying	Salt to taste

Method :

Boil, peel and mash the potatoes. Add besan and make it into a fine dough. Let it cool and divide it into 8 portions.

Boil peas. Mix with paneer and yellow colour. Divide this also into 8 portions.

Take on portion of paneer and cover it with potato paste. Make these into egg shaped koftas.

Heat oil and fry the koftas till brown.

Grind the onions and ginger. Take 2 tbsp. of oil and fry this paste till golden brown. Add chopped tomatoes and all the masalas. Fry it for 5 minutes. Add well beaten curd and half a cup of water. Let it simmer on low heat till gravy thickens. Put koftas in the gravy and remove from the heat immediately. Serve hot.

PALAK PANEER

Serves 4-6
Preparation Time 40 Minutes
Ingredients :

½ kg. palak	½ tsp. chilli powder
Paneer made from	¼ tsp. garam masala
4 cups of milk	½ tsp. garam masala
1 large onion	Oil for frying
1 cm. piece ginger	Salt to taste
2 tomatoes	2 tbsp. butter

Method :

Wash, cut and boil palak with salt and a little water for ten minutes. Grind it into a fine paste.

Heat oil. Cut paneer into 2 cm. cubical pieces and fry till light brown. Keep them aside.

Fry the finely chopped ginger and onion in two tbsp. oil till golden brown. Add chilli powder, turmeric powder and pieces of tomatoes. Cook them for 2-3 minutes. Add palak and half a cup of water. Let it simmer for 10 minutes. Add paneer pieces and let it remain on low heat for another five minutes. Add butter, sprinkle garam masala and serve hot.

SHAHI PANEER

Serves 4-6

Preparation Time 30 Minutes

Ingredients :

Paneer made from	1 cup thick curd
six cups of milk	15 cashew nuts
2 large onions	½ tsp. chilli powder
1 cm. piece ginger	½ tsp. garam masala
6 cloves of garlic	¼ tsp. turmeric powder
2 large tomatoes	Salt to taste
2 tbsp. oil	tbsp. cream

Method :

Grind the onions, ginger and garlic into a fine paste. Heat oil. Brown the ground masala. Add chopped tomatoes, turmeric, chilli powder and salt. Cook it for five minutes. Add well beaten curd and garam masala. Let it simmer on low heat till the gravy is thick.

Cut the paneer into thin rectangular pieces. Keep them in a shallow serving dish. Pour hot gravy over it. Decorate with cream and cashew nuts and serve immediately.

PANEER KOFTAS

Serves 4-6
Preparation Time 40 Minutes
Ingredients :

Paneer made from	½ cup thick curd
four cups of milk	½ tsp. chilli powder
2 small boiled potatoes	½ tsp. garam masala
1 tbsp. maida	¼ tsp. turmeric powder
2 large onions	Salt to taste
1 cm. piece ginger	½ tsp. dhania powder
2 large tomatoes	Oil for frying

Method :

Mash the boiled potatoes and mix with mashed paneer and maida. Mash them nicely at least for 5 minutes. Add a pinch of salt. Make into lemon sized balls.

Heat oil and fry the koftas till brown in colour. Keep them aside.

Grind the onions and ginger to a fine paste. Heat 2 tbsp. oil and fry this ground masala till brown. Add chopped tomatoes, salt, turmeric powder, dhania and chillis. Fry for 5 minutes. Add well beaten curd and one cup of water to it. Let it simmer on low heat till the gravy is thick. Add the koftas and remove from heat. Serve immediately.

LAUKI KOFTAS

Serves 4-6
Preparation Time 30 Minutes

Ingredients :

250 gm. lauki	Oil for frying
4 tbsp. besan	¼ tsp. turmeric powder
2 large onions	½ tsp. chilli powder
1 cm. piece ginger	½ tsp. dhania powder
6 cloves of garlic	½ tsp. garam masala
2 large tomatoes	Salt to taste

Method :

Peel, wash and grate the lauki. Add besan, a pinch of red chilli powder and ½ tsp. salt. Mix well and make into lemon sized balls. Heat oil in a karahi and fry these koftas 4-6 at a time on low heat till they are golden brown in colour.

Grind the onions, ginger and garlic to a fine paste. Fry this masala in 2 tbsp. of oil. When brown add tomato pieces, turmeric, chilli powder, dhania powder and salt. Cook for 5 minutes. Add one cup of water and bring it to boil Let it simmer on the low heat till the gravy thickens. Put koftas in it and boil for another two minutes. Sprinkle garam masala and serve hot.

BANANA KOFTAS

Serves 4-6
Preparation Time 40 Minutes

Ingredients :

2 large raw bananas	1 cm. piece ginger
2 potatoes	¼ tsp. turmeric powder
(medium size)	½ tsp. garam masala
2 tbsp. besan	½ tsp. chilli powder
2 large tomatoes	¼ tsp. ajwain
6 cloves of garlic	Salt to taste
2 large onions	Oil for frying

Method :

Boil bananas and potatoes till tender. Remove skin and mash these to a smooth paste. Add besan, ajwain and a pinch of salt. Mix well and make into lemon size balls. Heat oil and deep fry the koftas till golden brown.

Grind the onions, ginger and garlic into a fine paste. Heat oil. Fry ground masala till brown. Add chopped tomatoes and chilli powder. Fry for sometime. Add three cups of water. Bring it to boil and reduce the heat. Let it simmer till the gravy thickens. Add koftas and garam masala. Boil for two minutes and serve immediately.

KAMAL KAKRI KOFTAS

Serves 4-6
Preparation Time 40 Minutes

Ingredients :

250 gm. kamal kakri	2 large tomatoes
2 tbsp. besan	½ tsp. turmeric powder
2 large onions	½ tsp. chilli powder
1 cm. piece ginger	½ tsp. garam masala
6 cloves of garlic	Oil for frying
Pinch of hing	Salt to taste
10-12 dried plums	

Method :

Cut the kamal kakri in small pieces and wash them thoroughly. Grind it into a coarse paste. Add hing, besan and a little salt. Mix well and make into lemon size balls. Put one plum in the centre of each ball. Fry in oil till golden brown in colour.

Grind the onions, ginger and garlic into a fine paste. Fry ground masala in 2 tbsp. of oil till brown in colour. Add chopped tomatoes, salt, turmeric and chilli powder. Fry for a few minutes. Add 3 cups of water. Bring it to boil and reduce the heat. Let it simmer for 10 minutes. Add koftas and boil for 5 minutes. Add garam masala and serve hot.

Chapter VI
Dry Vegetable
Dishes

VEGETABLE KEEMA

Serves 4-6
Preparation Time 30 Minutes

Ingredients :

1/2 kg. cauliflower (Gobi)
1 cup shelled peas
1 large onion
1 cm. piece ginger
5-6 cloves garlic
2 green chillis
2 large tomatoes
Salt to taste

2 tbsp. chopped cashewnuts
2 tbsp. kishmish
¼ tsp. turmeric powder
½ tsp. chilli powder
½ tsp. dhania powder
½ tsp. garam masala
4 tbsp. oil

Method :

Boil the peas with a pinch of salt till tender.
Wash and great the cauliflower. Heat 2 tbsp. oil and fry gobi till light brown.

Heat the remaining oil. Fry chopped onions, ginger, garlic and green chillis till light brown in colour. Add chopped tomatoes, salt, dhania powder, turmeric and chilli powder. Fry for 2-3 minutes. Add fried gobi, mattar, kishmish and half of the cashewnuts. Cook for 5 minutes.

Serve in a shallow dish with remaining cashewnuts at the top.

STUFFED CAPSICUM

Serves 4-6

Preparation Time 40 Minutes

Ingredients :

8 medium size capsicums	1 tbsp. oil
6 medium size potatoes	½ tsp. chilli powder
1 small onion	½ tsp. dhania powder
Salt to taste	½ tsp. garam masala
	¼ tsp. amchur

Method :

Boil the potatoes till tender. Peel and mash them. Mix all the masalas and finely chopped onions.

Cut out a slice from the top of each capsicum. Remove the seeds and stuff them with the potato mixture. Smear oil around the capsicum. Heat remaining oil in a karahi (deep frying pan). Place the capsicums in it . Cover them and cook on low heat for 10-15 minutes, turning them occasionally until they are tender and light brown in colour.

Serve in a shallow serving dish. Decorate with onion and tomato rings.

You can stuff capsicums with boiled channa dal or moong dal also.

STUFFED KARELAS I

Serves 4-6

Preparation Time 40 Minutes

Ingredients :

8 large green karelas	½ tsp. chilli powder
6 large potatoes	½ tsp. garam masala
1 large onion	½ tsp. dhania powder
Salt to taste	1tsp. amchur
oil for frying	

Method :

Scrape the karelas. Slit them on one side and remove the seeds. Apply salt generously inside and outside them. Keep for 2-3 hours. Wash them thoroughly and squeeze them to remove the water.

Boil, peel and mash the potatoes. Mix with chopped onions and all the masalas. Fill this mixture in the karelas. Wrap them with cotton thread so that mixture remains intact while frying.

Heat oil in a karai. Fry the karelas on a low heat till these are golden brown. Remove the thread before serving.

STUFFED KARELAS II

Serves 4-6
Preparation Time 40 Minutes

Ingredients :

8 large green karelas	1/2 tsp. chilli powder
1 cup besan	1/2 tsp. garam masala
1 large onion	1 tsp. ground anardana
Salt to taste	1 tsp. dhania powder
	Oil for frying

Method :

Scrape and prepare the karelas as in the previous recipe.

Heat 1/2 tbsp. oil in a karahi. Fry beasn on low heat till light brown in colour. Mix all the masalas and finely chopped onions with besan. Fill this mixture in the karelas and wrap them with thread.

Heat the remaining oil in a karahi and fry the karelas till golden brown in colour. Remove the threads before serving.

STUFFED BHINDIS

Serves 4-6

Preparation Time 20 Minutes

Ingredients :

250 gm. long tender bhindis	1tsp. dhania powder
1 tbsp. besan	½ tsp. chilli powder
½ tsp. amchur	½ tsp. turmeric powder
Salt to taste	½ tsp. garam masala
	2 tbsp. oil

Method :

Wash and dry the bhindis with a clean napkin. Remove the heads and slit them lengthwise on one side.

Mix all the masala with besan and fill the bhindes with it.

Heat oil in a karahi and fry bhindis for 2-3 minutes turning continuously. Reduce the heat and cover them. Cook for 2-3 minutes. Now remove the cover. Fry the bhindis for another 4-5 minutes on low heat stirrring occasionally till bhindis are soft and leave the oil.

MASALA BAIGAN

Serves 4-6
Preparation Time 20 Minutes

Ingredients :

250 gm. small round
baigan of equal size
1 tsp. dhania powder
½ tsp. turmeric powder
¼ tsp. ground pepper

½ tsp. chilli powder
1 tsp. amchur
Salt to taste
2 tbsp. oil

Method :

Wash and dry the brinjals. Cut 1 cm. piece of brinjals from the stem side. Slit each of them on one side only.

Mix all the masalas and fill into brinjals.

Heat oil in a karahi. Fry the brinjals for 2-3 minutes turning continuously. Reduce the heat and cover them with a lid. Cook them until soft. Remove the lid and cook for another 3-4 minutes till it leaves oil.

FRIED BAIGANS

Serves 4-6
Preparation Time 15 Minutes

Ingredients :

2 large round brinjals	½ chilli powder
Salt to taste	1 tsp. amchur.
oil for frying	2 tbsp. grated paneer
	1 bunch coriander leaves

Method :

Wash and dry the brinjals. Cut them into 1 to 2 cm thick round slices.

Heat oil in a karahi, Fry 3-4 pieces at a time until brown on both the sides. It takes two or three minutes to get these brown and soft.

Mix all the masalas and sprinkle over the brinjals. Arrange in a shallow serving dish. Garnish with coriander leaves and paneer. Serve hot.

BAIGAN BHARTA

Serves 4-6
Preparation Time 30 Minutes

Ingredients :

1 large round brinjal	2 tbsp oil
(about 250 gm)	1 tsp. chilli powder
3 large onions	1 bunch coriander leaves
3 medium size tomatoes	1 tbsp butter
½ cup shelled peas	

Method :

Grease the brinjal lightly. Place over the gas burners with high heat till the skin becomes black and it is soft inside.

Remove the skin, wash and mash it well.

Heat oil in a frying pan. Fry the finely chopped onions till light brown in colour. Add the peas and chopped tomatoes. Cook them for another 2-3 minutes. Add the mashed brinjal, salt and chilli powder. Cook for 5-10 minutes until it leaves the oil. Mix butter to it.

Garnish with coriander leaves and serve hot.

TURNIP BHARTA

Serves 4-6
Preparation Time 30 Minutes

Ingredients :

½ kg. tender white turnips	Salt to taste
1 cm. piece ginger	½ tsp. turmeric powder
1 bunch coriander leaves	½ tsp. chilli powder
2 tbsp. oil	¼ tsp. ground pepper
1 tbsp. butter	1 tsp. sugar
2 green chillis	

Method :

Wash, peel and cut the turnips into small pieces. Boil with 1/4 cup of water and salt till they are tender and water is dried up. Mash it.

Heat oil. Put mashed turnips, green chillis, ginger, sugar and all the masalas. Cook for 5-10 minutes until it leaves oil. Mix in butter.

Garnish with coriander leaves and serve hot.

GOBI MUSSALAM

Serves 4-6
Preparation Time 40 Minutes

Ingredients :

One medium size
cauliflower

2 large onions

1 cm. piece ginger

2 green chillis

2 large tomatoes

4 tbsp. oil

½ tsp. garam masala

1 tsp. dhania powder

½ tsp. chilli powder

½ tsp. turmeric powder

Salt to taste

1 bunch coriander leaves

2 tbsp. grated paneer

Method :

Take only the flower of gobi. Boil it in the salted water for 5 minutes. Take it out of the water and keep aside.

Heat oil and fry chopped onions, ginger and green chillis. Fry for 5 minutes. Add chopped tomatoes, chilli powder, dhania, turmeric powder and salt. Fry for another 5 minutes.

Keep the gobi upside down. Fill it with fried masala. Smear the remaining masala all around the gobi. Cook it in a shallow frying pan in upright position till water dries up.

Serve whole, garnished with coriander leaves and grated paneer.

STUFFED TOMATOES

Serves 4-6
Preparation Time 40 Minutes

Ingredients :

8 medium sized
ripe tomatoes
4 medium size
potatoes
2 tbsp. shelled peas

1 tbsp. oil
½ tsp. garam masala
½ tsp. chilli powder
Salt to taste
1 small bunch of
coriander leaves

Method :

Boil the potatoes till tender. Boil peas with a little salt separately just for two minutes Mash the potatoes. Mix with peas and all the masalas and coriander leaves.

Cut out a slice from the top of each tomato. Scoop out the pulp and stuff the tomatoes with potatoes and peas mixture. Smear the tomatoes with oil. Heat a shallow frying pan.

Put the stuffed tomatoes in the pan and cook covered on low heat for two minutes. Turn them and cook for another two minutes.

Serve in a shallow serving dish. Decorate with onion rings.

These tomatoes can be stuffed with peas and paneer mixture also.

MASALA KATHAL

Serves 4-6
Preparation Time 45 Minutes

Ingredients :

½ kg. kathal (Jack- fruit)	½ tsp. turmeric powder
3 large onions	½ tsp. chilli powder
2 large tomatoes	1 tsp. dhania powder
2 green chillies	1 tsp. garam masala
1 cm. piece ginger	½ cup of beaten curd
6 cloves of garlic	4 tbsp oil
Salt to taste	

Method :

Peel and cut the kathal into small pieces. Heat 2 tbsp. oil in a karahi and fry the kathal till golden brown.
Heat the remaining oil. Add chopped onions, ginger, garlic and green chillis. Fry till light brown in colour. Now add chopped tomatoes and all the masalas. Cook for two minutes. Add fried kathal. Cook it covered on a very low heat till jack-fruit is tender. Add curd and cook for another 4-5 minutes till well mixed.

MASALA ARBI

Serves 4-6
Preparation Time 40 Minutes

Ingredients :

½ kg. arbi of equal size   ½ tsp. turmeric powder
2 large onions   ½ tsp. chilli powder
2 large tomatoes   1½ tsp. dhania powder
1 small piece ginger   ½ tsp. garam masala
8 green chillis   Salt to taste
2 tbsp. oil

Method :

Peel and wash the arbi. Dry it with a napkin. Slit them on one side. Slit 6 green chillies also on one side. Mix dhania, garam masala, 1/4 tsp. chilli powder, 1/4 tsp. turmeric powder and salt together. Fill all the arbi and chillis with this dry masala.

Heat oil Fry chopped onions, ginger and green chillis till light brown in colour. Add chopped tomatoes, remaining chilli powder, salt and turmeric powder and cook for 3-4 minutes. Now put the arbi. Fry for 5 minutes stirring continuously. Put 1/2 cup of water and cook covered on a very low heat till the arbi is tender and water dries up.

ARBI FRY

Serves 4-6
Preparation Time 20 Minutes

Ingredients :

½ kg. arbi (big pieces)   Salt to taste
½ tsp. ajwain   ½ tsp. chilli powder
Oil for frying   1tsp. amchur
½ tsp. garam masala

Method :

Boil the arbi till tender. Remove the skin and let it cool for about half an hour. Flatten each piece by pressing with hand.

Heat oil in a karahi. Deep fry few pieces at a time till golden brown in colour.

Sprinkle all the masalas while the arbi is still hot and serve.

ALU DO PYAJA

Serves 4-6
Preparation Time 20 Minutes

Ingredients :

250 gm. medium sized potatoes

4 medium sized onions

4 medium sized tomatoes

2 green chillis

1 cm. piece ginger

6 cloves of garlic

½ tsp. chilli powder

½ tsp. turmeric powder

1 tsp. dhania powder

½ tsp. garam masala

Salt to taste

2 tbsp. oil

Method :

Boil and peel the potatoes. Cut them into round pieces of 1 cm. thickness. Cut the onions also in thick rings.

Heat oil. Fry the onions for two minutes. Add potato pieces and chopped green chillis. Fry for another two minutes. Now add the chopped tomatoes and all other masalas except garam masala. Cook uncovered for five minutes till it leaves oil. Sprinkle garam masala and serve hot.

SHAHI ALU

Serves 4-6
Preparation Time 30 Minutes

Ingredients :

4 large potatoes
½ cup paneer
½ cup shelled peas
1 bunch coriander leaves
2 tbsp. kishmish
8 almonds

Salt to taste
¼ tsp. chilli powder
¼ tsp. ground pepper
oil for frying
1 tomato

Method :

Peel, wash and cut the potatoes into half lengthwise. Scoop out the potato halves leaving about 1 cm. thick shell. Smear with salt and keep for 5 minutes. Wash and dry with a napkin.

Boil the peas with little water till tender. Mix peas with paneer, kishmish, coriander leaves and masalas.

Fry the potatoes on low heat until they are golden brown in colour and tender.

Fill the empty portion of potatoes with peas and paneer mixture.

Serve in a shallow serving dish. Decorate with sliced almonds and tomato rings.

SUKHEY ALU

Serves 4-6
Preparation Time 15 Minutes

Ingredients :

½ kg. potatoes	½ tsp. chilli powder
2 tbsp. oil. (preferably mustard oil)	1 tsp. dhania powder
	½ tsp. garam masala
Salt to taste	½ tsp. amchur
A pinch of hing	½ tsp. jeera

Method :

Boil, peel and cut the potatoes into half or quarter. Heat oil. Put jeera, hing and dhania powder. Fry for 2 minutes. Now put potato pieces and all the other masalas. Cook uncovered on low heat for about 5 minutes stirring continuously.

These potatoes can be kept for 3-4 days without fridge.

MATTAR DO PYAJA

Serves 4-6
Preparation Time 20 Minutes

Ingredients :

2 cups shelled peas
4 large onions
2 green chillies
1 cm. piece of ginger
8 cloves of garlic
2 tbsp. oil

¼ tsp. turmeric powder
½ tsp. chilli powder
1 tsp. dhania powder
½ tsp. garam masala
Salt to taste
1 bunch coriander leaves.

Method :

Cut the onions lengthwise into big pieces. Chop garlic, ginger and green chillis.

Heat oil. Put all the vegetables and masalas except garam masala. Mix well and cook in pressure cooker for one whistle only. Mix lightly.

Sprinkle garam masala and garnish with coriander leaves.

CABBAGE WITH PEAS

Serves 4-6
Preparation Time 20 Minutes

Ingredients :

½ kg. cabbage	1 tsp. dhania powder
1 cup shelled peas	½ tsp. chilli powder
1 large onion	½ tsp. garam masala
2 green chillis	¼ tsp. turmeric powder
1 cm. piece of ginger	Salt to taste
1 large tomato	1 tbsp. oil

Method :

Wash and finely chop the cabbage. Chop onion, chillis and ginger.

Heat oil. Fry chopped onion, chillis and ginger for 2-3 minutes. Add chopped tomatoes and all the masalas. Fry for a few minutes. Now add cabbage and peas. Cover and cook on medium heat till peas are tender and water dries up.

Sprinkle with garam masala.

STUFFED LAUKI

Serves 4-6
Preparation Time 40 Minutes

Ingredients :

One small tender lauki (about ½ kg.)
4 large potatoes
½ cup shelled peas
½ cup small cubes of paneer
1 bunch coriander leaves
1 tsp. chilli powder
½ tsp. garam masala
1 tsp. dhania powder
Salt to taste
1 tbsp. oil
2 green chillis

Method :

Scrape lauki and cut lengthwise into two equal pieces. Scoop out the seeds. Boil water in a saucepan with a little salt. Put the lauki in it, cover it and cook for two minutes. Remove from heat and let the lauki remain in water for about half an hour.

Boil peas in salted water for 5 minutes.
Boil, peel and mash the potatoes. Add chopped green chillis, coriander leaves, peas, paneer and all the masalas to potatoes. Fill both the pieces of lauki with this mixture. Smear oil around the lauki.

Heat remaining oil in a karahi. Fry this lauki for a few minutes on both the sides. Serve in a shallow dish and decorate with tomato and onion rings.

MIXED VEGETABLES

Serves 4-6
Preparation Time 30 Minutes

Ingredients :

½ cup shelled peas
1 large potato
100 gm. cauliflower
100 gm. carrots
100 gm. french beans
1 onion
1 large tomato
2 green chillis
1 cm. piece ginger

2 tsp. dhania powder
1 tsp. chilli powder
½ tsp. turmeric powder
½ tsp. garam masala
Salt to taste
2 tbsp. oil
1 bunch coriander leaves

Method :

Wash and cut all the vegetables into very small pieces.

Heat oil. Put the chopped vegetables except tomato. Add salt, dhania powder, chilli and turmeric powder Mix them well. Cover and cook on medium heat stirring occasionally till the vegetables are tender and water dries up. Add tomatoes and cook for another 2-3 minutes. Sprikle garam masala.

Garnish with coriander leaves and serve hot.

Chapter VII
Curd
Preparations

DAHI PAKORIS

Serves 4-6
Preparation Time 50 Minutes

Ingredients :

1 cup moong dal (green gram dal without husk)
½ kg. thick curd
Oil for frying
1 cup saunth
1 tsp. Kala namak

1 tsp. jeera powder
½ tsp. chilli powder
½ tsp. pepper powder
2 tbsp. salt

Method :

Soak the dal overnight in enough water. Wash and drain. Grind it into a very find paste without adding water. Beat it with hand till it is fluffy. Add a little water if necessary.

Heat oil in a karahi. Fry 8-10 pakoris of lemon size at a time till golden brown.

Add salt in water and soak these pakoris for about an hour. Remove from water and press lightly.

Beat the curd. Add salt, chilli powder, pepper and kala namak. Put the pakoris in curd. Sprinkle jeera and chilli powder over it. Serve with saunth.

BOONDI RAITA

Serves 4-6
Preparation Time 30 Minutes

Ingredients :

½ cup besan	¼ tsp. chilli powder
250 gm. curd	¼ tsp. pepper powder
Oil for frying	½ tsp. jeera powder
1 bunch coriander leaves	¼ tsp. kala namak
	Salt to taste

Method :

Prepare a thick batter of besan adding about one cup of water and a little salt. Beat well till fluffy.

Heat oil. Pour a little batter through a shallow spoon having round holes. It will fall like drops in oil. Fry till golden. Soak the boondi in water for about 10 minutes.

Beat the curd and add all the masalas. Take out the boondi from water and squeeze to drain out water and put into curd. Decorate with chopped coriander leaves. Cool it before serving.

LAUKI RAITA

Serves 4-6

Preparation Time 15 Minutes

Ingredients :

200 gm. lauki   ½ tsp. jeera powder
½ kg. curd   ½ tsp. pepper powder
Salt to taste   ¼ tsp. chilli powder
¼ tsp. kala namak

Method :

Peel and grate the lauki. Boil it with a little water for 5 minutes. Drain out the water if there is any and let it cool.

Beat the curd. Put all the masalas and the boiled lauki. Sprinkle jeera over it. Cool it before serving.

KHEERA RAITA

Serves 4-6
Preparation Time 10 Minutes

Ingredients :

2 medium sized kheeras
½ kg. curd
Salt to taste
¼ tsp. pepper powder

¼ tsp. chilli powder
½ tsp. jeera powder
½ tsp. kala namak

Method :

Peel and grate the kheeras. Remove excess water, if any.

Beat the curd. Add all the masalas and grated kheera. Sprinkle jeera powder over it. Cool it before serving.

POTATO RAITA

Serves 4-6
Preparation Time 15 Minutes

Ingredients :

2 large potatoes
½ kg. curd
1 bunch pudina
Salt to taste
2 green chillis

¼ tsp. chilli powder
½ tsp. jeera powder
¼ tsp. pepper
½ tsp. kala namak

Method :

Boil, peel and cut the potatoes into small cubes.
Chop green chillis and pudina.

Beat the curd. Add potatoes, green chillis, pudina
and all the masalas.
Cool and serve.

RAITA-SWEET AND SOUR

Serves 4-6
Preparation Time 20 Minutes

Ingredients :

2 ripe bananas
2 green chillis
2 tbsp. kishmish
1 orange
2 slices of pineapple
Salt to taste

½ tsp. jeera powder
¼ tsp. chilli powder
½ tsp. pepper powder
½ kg. curd

Method :

Peel and cut the bananas, pineapple and orange into small pieces. Chop the green chillis. Wash the kishmish and soak in water for about 10 minutes.

Beat the curd. Add all the masalas, fruit and chopped chillis. Cool it before serving.

DAHI BHALLAS

Serves 4-6
Preparation Time 50 Minutes

Ingredients :

1 cup urd dal without husk	½ tsp. chilli powder
½ kg. thick curd.	½ tsp. pepper powder
Oil for frying	1 tsp. jeera
1 cm. piece ginger	1 tsp. kala namak
2 tbsp. kishmish	2 tbsp. salt
	1 cup saunth

Method :

Soak the dal overnight. Wash and remove the water. Grind it into a very find paste without adding water. Beat it with hand till it is fluffy. A little water can be added while beating if required. Mix chopped ginger and kishmish.

Heat oil in a karahi. Take a little dal paste (about 1 tbsp.) and flatten it on your wet palm. Fry this in the oil till golden brown. 6-7 bhallas can be fried at a time.

Add salt in water and soak all the bhallas in it. Leave these for ½ hour.

Take out the bhallas from water and press them with hand lightly to remove water. Arrange in a shallow serving dish.

Beat the curd. Mix kala namak, pepper and chilli powder. Keep in a cool place.

Roast and grind the jeera. Add half of it in the curd. Pour the curd over the bhallas. Sprinkle jeera and chilli powder. Serve with saunth.

PALAK RAITA

Serves 4-6
Preparation Time 20 Minutes

Ingredients :

250 gm. palak	¼ tsp. chilli powder
½ kg. curd	¼ tsp. pepper powder
Salt to taste	½ tsp. kala namak
2 green chillis	½ tsp. jeera powder

Method :

Take palak leaves and wash and chop them finely. Boil with very little water for 5 minutes. Remove the water if any and let it cool.

Beat the curd. Add chopped green chillis and the masalas. Put the palak and mix well.
Cool it before serving.

MIXED VEGETABLE RAITA

Serves 4-6
Preparation Time 20 Minutes

Ingredients :

2 small carrots — ½ kg. curd
1 small kheera — ¼ tsp. chilli powder
4 small potatoes — ½ tsp. pepper powder
1 small onion — 1 tsp. jeera powder
2 small tomatoes — Salt to taste
2 green chillis — 1 bunch coriander leaves

Method :

Boil, peel and cut the potatoes into small pieces. Cut the carrots into small pieces and boil with a little water till tender. Chop the other vegetables also.

Beat the curd and add the masalas. Add all the vegetables to the curd and mix. Cool and serve.

Traditional Indian Cooking

QUICK DAHI KADHI

Serves 4-6
Preparation Time 15 Minutes

Ingredients :

2 cups well beaten curd   Salt to taste
2 tbsp. besan   ½ tsp. mustard seeds
1 medium size onion   ½ tsp. jeera
6 dried red chillies   ¼ tsp. chilli powder
1 tbsp. oil   ¼ tsp. turmeric powder
1 bunch curry leaves

Method :

Heat oil. Put jeera and mustard seeds. Add chopped onions, curry leaves and whole red chillis. Slow the heat, put besan and fry till light brown in colour. Add all the masalas.

Pour curd and ½ cup of water over this mixture. Mix well, bring it to boil and remove from heat.

Serve hot.

KADHI WITH PAKORAS

Serves 4-6
Preparation Time 50 Minutes

Ingredients :

For Kadhi
½ kg. sour curd
¼ tsp. jeera
¼ methi seeds
½ tsp. garam masala
1 bunch coriander leaves
4 tbsp. besan
Salt to taste
1 tsp. chilli powder
½ tsp. turmeric powder

For Pakoras
4 tbsp. besan
½ tsp. red chilli
Salt to taste
Oil for frying
1 large onion
4 green chillis
1 cm. piece ginger
8 cloves of garlic

Method :

Chop the onions, ginger, garlic and chillis finely. Make a thick but smooth batter of besan, chopped vegetables, salt and red chillis. Beat it well.

Heat oil in a karahi. Fry 8-10 lemon sized pakoras at a time till golden brown. Use all the besan and keep the pakoras aside.

Beat the curd. Add 5 cups of water. Add besan, salt, chilli powder and turmeric powder. Beat it well.

Heat 1 tbsp. oil in a heavy bottomed pan. Put jeera

and methi seeds. Pour curd mixture and bring it to boil stirring continuously. Reduce the heat and cook for about 15 minutes stirring occasionally.

Now add the pakoras and cook for another 10 minutes. Sprinkle garam masala and chopped coriander leaves over it.

Serve hot.

Chapter - VIII
Sweets And
Sweet Dishes

RICE KHEER

Serves 4-6
Preparation Time 45 Minutes

Ingredients :

1 litre thick milk   20 almonds
½ cup sugar   2 tbsp. kishmish
3 tbsp. basmati rice   5 green cardamoms

Method :

Wash and soak the rice in water for about half an hour.

Boil milk in a thick bottomed pan. Put the rice. Bring it to boil and reduce the heat. Cook until the rice is well cooked. Mix thoroughly with a big spoon. Cook for another 5 minutes stirring it continuously.

Add sugar, chopped almonds, kishmish and crushed cardamom seeds. Mix well.

Serve hot or chilled, as desired.

SEVIA KHEER

Serves 4-6
Preparation Time 25 Minutes

Ingredients :

1 litre milk	10 almonds
1 cup very fine sevia	2 tbsp. kishmish
½ cup sugar	5 green cardamoms

Method :

Roast servia till golden brown.

Boil milk. Put sevia in it and bring it to boil. Reduce the heat and cook for 10 minutes. Mix with a spoon and cook for another 5 minutes stirring it continuously.

Add sugar, kishmish, chopped almonds and crushed cardamom seeds. Mix well.

Serve hot or chilled.

CARROT KHEER

Serves 4-6
Preparation Time 40 Minutes

Ingredients :

250 gm. carrots	10 cashewnuts
1 litre milk	2 tbsp. kishmish
½ cup sugar	5 green cardamoms

Method :

Wash, peel and grate the carrots. Add milk and bring it to boil. Reduce the heat and cook till milk reduces to half in volume. Add sugar and cook for another five minutes.

Add chopped cashewnuts, kishmish and seeds of cardamoms.

Serve hot or chilled.

PANEER KHEER

Serves 4-6
Preparation Time 30 Minutes

Ingredients :

1 litre milk	10 almonds
200 gm. paneer	5 green cardamoms
½ cup sugar	15-20 makhaney
	1 tsp. ghee

Method :

Heat ghee and fry makhaney till golden. Crush them coarsely.

Cut paneer into very small cubes. Boil milk till it reduces to half. Add paneer and makhaney and let it boil on slow heat for 15 minutes. Add sugar and bring it to boil.

Add chopped almonds and crushed cardamom seeds.

Serve chilled.

RABRI

Serves 4-6
Preparation Time   50 Minutes

Ingredients :

2 litres milk	5 green cardamoms
1 cup sugar	15 almonds
2 tsp. rose water	15 pistachios

Method :

Take a karahi. Pour milk in it and bring it to boil. Reduce the heat to medium level. Boil it stirring frequently in the centre and keeping the cream on the sides of the karahi.

When the milk evaporates to one-fourth volume, add sugar and crushed cardamom seeds. Cook for another 5 minutes. Remove all the cream from the sides and mix well with the thickened milk.

Cool. it. Add chopped almonds and pistachios. Keep in the refrigerator. Add rose water before serving.

FALOODA

Serves 4-6
Preparation Time 40 Minutes

Ingredients :

4 tbsp. cornflour
          or
4 tbsp. arrowroot flour
2 cups rabri
    Crushed ice

½ cup Rooh-Afza
or rose sharbat
1½ cups water

Method :

Add ½ cup of water in the cornflour to make a smooth paste. Boil the remaining 1 cup of water in a thick pan. Add cornflour paste to it. Cook it stirring continuously till it is transparent and very thick. Let it cool down for some time.

Take chilled water in a pan. Put some of the cornflour paste in a sevia making machine. Press it. Long strings of falooda will fall in the water. Keep the falooda in chilled water only.

Serve falooda with rabri and crushed ice after pouring sharbat over it.

RASGULLA

Serves 4-6
Preparation Time 50 Minutes

Ingredients :

1½ litres thick milk	2½ cups sugar
½ cup sour curd	4 cups water
	2 tbsp. rose water

Method :

Boil milk. Add curd boil and till the milk curdles up. Strain through a muslin cloth. Wash this paneer for 2-3 minutes under running water. Press paneer under a heavy stone for 2-3 hours.

Take the paneer in a tray. Mash it well and knead with the palm of your hand for about 15 minutes till it becomes soft the creamy. Make balls of the size of walnuts and keep aside.

Take water and sugar in a big saucepan. Bring it to boil. Put the paneer balls in it in single layer only. Cover it and boil for 10 minutes. Reduce heat and sprinkle some water over rasgullas. Boil for another 10 minutes. At the end they should be double in size and spongy in appearance.

Cool along with the syrup in the fridge for 5-6 hours. Sprinkle rose water just before serving.

RASMALAI

Serves 4-6
Preparation Time 50 Minutes

Ingredients :

1 litre milk for making
paneer
750 ml milk for malai
½ cup sour curd
5 green cardamoms

2½ cups sugar
10 almonds
10 pistachios
A pinch of saffron

Method :

Make paneer with 1 litre of milk and curd. Make balls of paneer as in the recipe of rasgullas. Flatten the balls and keep aside.

Make syrup with 2 cups of sugar and 3½ cups of water. Bring it to boil. Put the rasgullas in single layer, and boil for 10 minutes. They should swell up at the end and should be double in size. Take these out from the syrup.

Boil the 750 ml of milk. Take out one cup of milk in a pan and soak the rasgullas in it for 5-6 hours. Keep on boiling the remaining milk till it is very thick like rabri. Add half a cup of sugar and boil for another 1 minute.

Take out the rasgullas from the milk. Put these in

a shallow serving dish. Mix the rabri with the milk. Pour over the rasgullas to make rasmalais.

Sprinkle crushed cardamom seeds. Decorate with chopped almonds, pistachios and saffron. Cool and serve.

GULAB JAMUN (NO. 1)

Serves 4-6
Preparation Time 40 Minutes

Ingredients :

2 cups whole milk powder

½ cup maida

2½ tbsp. oil for dough

¼ tsp. baking powder

¼ cup liquid milk

2 cups sugar

3 cups water

4 green cardamoms

Oil for frying

Method :

Sieve maida and baking powder together. Put milk powder and 2½ tbsp. of oil in it. Mix it well with hand for 5 minutes. Now make a soft dough adding liquid milk in it. Make balls of the size of walnuts from the dough.

Heat oil in a karahi. Fry these balls on medium heat turning continuously until they are dark brown in colour.

Boil water and sugar. Add crushed cardamoms. Boil for 5 minutes. Add the gulab jamuns and boil for 10 minutes on medium heat.

Let the gulab jamuns remain in syrup for 4-5 hours. Heat them again before serving.

Traditional Indian Cooking

GULAB JAMUN (NO. 2)

Serves 4-6
Preparation Time 40 Minutes

Ingredients :

250 gm. khoya
½ cup maida
A pinch of baking
powder
½ tbsp. oil for dough
2 tbsp. liquid milk

2 cups sugar
3 cups water
4 green cardamoms
Oil for frying

Method :

Sieve maida and baking powder together and add oil. Break up the khoya into granules. Mix all these ingredients well with your hand. Add liquid milk and make a soft and smooth dough. Knead well for about 5 minutes. Make balls of the size of walnuts.

Heat oil. Fry these balls on a medium heat till dark brown in colour.

Boil water and sugar. Add crushed cardamoms. Boil for 5 minutes. Add gulab jamuns and boil for 10 minutes on medium heat.

Let the gulab jamuns remain in syrup for 4-5 hours. Heat them again before serving.

FIRNI

Serves 6-8

Preparation Time 40 Minutes

Ingredients :

1 litre milk

½ cup rice or rice powder

1 cup sugar

5 green cardamoms

10 pistachios

20 almonds

2 tbsp. kishmish

¼ tsp. kesar

Method :

Wash and soak the rice in water for about half an hour. Grind to a very fine paste adding a little water. Add water to make 1½ cups of this rice milk. Keep aside. Soak kesar in 2 tbsp. of milk.

Boil milk in a thick bottomed pan. Add rice milk. If rice powder is used, add water to make into 1½ cups liquid. Boil milk and rice milk mixture on medium heat stirring continuously till the mixture thickens. Add sugar, kishmish and half of the crushed cardamom seeds. Boil for another five minutes. Add Kesar.

Pour firni immediately into ice cream bowls or sakoras (earthenware cups). Decorate with chopped almonds, pistachios and remaining crushed cardamom seeds.

Cool it in refrigerator for 3-4 hours before serving. In winter, it can be served hot also.

Traditional Indian Cooking

SWEET SEVIA

Serves 4-6
Preparation Time 30 Minutes

Ingredients :

1 packet thick
sevia (250 gm)
2 tbsp oil
1 cup sugar
1 tbsp. butter

2 tbsp. kishmish
10 almonds
2 cups water

Method :

Heat oil in a deep frying pan. Fry sevia till light brown in colour. Add water and bring it to boil. Reduce the heat. Cover it and cook on a very low heat for 5 minutes. Now add sugar and kishmish. Cover and cook till the water dries up. Add butter and mix. Decorate with chopped almonds.

Serve hot.

SHAHI TOAST

Serves 4-6
Preparation Time 30 Minutes

Ingredients :

10 slices of bread
1 litre milk
½ cup sugar
Oil for frying

10 almonds
10 pistachios
4 green cardamoms

Method :

Cut the slices into halves. Heat oil in a karahi. Fry 5-6 pieces of bread at a time till golden brown.

Boil milk. Keep on boiling till it reduces to half. Add sugar and crushed cardamom seeds. Boil for another 2 minutes and remove from heat.

Dip fried slices in milk one by one and arrange them in a shallow serving dish. Pour the remaining milk over them. Decorate with chopped pista and almonds.

Cool in refrigerator before serving.

MALPURA

Serves 4-6
Preparation Time 30 Minutes

Ingredients :

1 cup suji	20 almonds
½ cup maida	2 tbsp. kishmish
½ cup curd	1 tsp. saunf
1 cup sugar	Oil for frying
½ cup milk	

Method :

Mix suji, maida, curd, milk and sugar. Beat it with a spoon adding water to make a smooth batter of pouring consistency.

Add saunf. kishmish and chopped almonds.

Heat oil in a frying pan. Pour 2 tbsp. of batter in oil. Fry it on medium heat till golden brown on both sides. Similarly fry remaining malpuras.

Serve hot.

CARROT HALWA

Serves 4-6
Preparation Time 60 Minutes

Ingredients :

1 kg. carrots   1½ cups sugars
2 litres milk or 1 litre   1 cup oil or ghee
milk and 250 gm. khoya or
4 cups of whole-milk powder
20 almonds
20 cashewnuts

Method :

Wash, scrape and grate the carrots. Add milk and keep on boiling till milk dries up. Add sugar and cook stirring continuously for 15-20 minutes. Add oil or ghee and cook till it becomes one lump and leaves the sides of the pan.

Add chopped almonds and cashewnuts.

Can be served hot or cold.

If milk powder is to be used, boil the carrots in half a cup of water till water dries up. Add powder and cook as given above.

If khoya is to be used, boil the carrots in one litre of milk and cook till milk dries up. Add khoya and cook as given above.

HALWA SUJI

Serves 4-6
Preparation Time 20 Minutes

Ingredients :

1 cup suji	2 tbsp. kishmish
1 cup sugar	20 almonds
1 cup oil or ghee	4 cups water

Method :

Mix sugar and water. Bring it to boil. Keep aside.

Heat oil or ghee in a deep frying pan. Fry suji in it till golden brown. Add sugar syrup and kishmish. Cook on high heat stirring continuously till it becomes one lump and leaves the sides of pan.

Decorate with chopped almonds and serve hot.

HALWA PETHA

Serves 4-6
Preparation Time 45 Minutes

Ingredients :

1 kg. petha (red marrow) 2 tbsp. kishmish
1 litre milk   20 almonds
1 cup sugar   4-5 green cardamoms
½ cup oil or ghee

Method :

Peel, wash and grate the petha. Add half cup of water and boil till tender. Add milk and keep on boiling till all the milk dries up. Add sugar and oil or ghee. Cook it stirring continuously till it becomes one lump and leaves the sides of the pan.

Add kishmish and chopped almonds.
Serve hot.

CHANNA OR MOONG DAL HALWA

Serves 4-6
Preparation Time 60 Minutes

Ingredients :

1 cup moong dal (without husk)
or channa dal
10 almonds
10 pistachios
10 cashew nuts
200 gm. khoya or
1 cup milk powder

1 cup oil or ghee
1 cup sugar
A pinch of yellow colour
(edible)

Method :

Soak dal over night. Grind it into a coarse paste with as little water as possible.

Heat oil or ghee. Fry the dal paste on low heat for about 20 minutes. Make syrup with sugar, yellow colour and 2 cups of water. Add this syrup to the fried dal. Cook till it becomes one lump and leaves the sides of the pan. Add khoya or milk powder and chopped dry fruit before serving.

Serve hot.

FRUIT CUSTARD WITH JELLY

Serves 4-6

Preparation Time 40 Minutes

Ingredients :

½ litre milk   4 bananas

2 tbsp. custard powder   1 orange

3 tbsp. sugar   1 apple

1 packet jelly crystals

(any flavour)

Method :

Boil two cups of water. Dissolve jelly crystals in it. Pour in a shallow dish and keep in the freezer for about ½ hour. When it sets keep in the chiller compartment of the fridge.

Mix custard powder with sugar and 4 tbsp. of cold milk. Boil the remaining milk. Put the custard and sugar mixture in it. Boil it stirring continuously till it is thick. Cool it completely.

Peel and cut the fruit into small pieces.

Mix half of the fruit with custard.

Take a shallow glass serving dish. Pour custard with fruit in it. Over it a layer of remaining fruit. Cut the set jelly into cubes and decorate over the fruit.

Keep it in the fridge for half an hour before serving.

JELLY WITH FRUIT & CREAM

Serves **4-6**

Preparation Time 30 Minutes

Ingredients :

1 packet jelly crystals	1 orange
2 large ripe mangoes	1 apple
or 4 bananas	
½ cup fresh cream	

Method :

Make jelly with 2 cups of boiling water. Let it cool down.

Peel and cut the fruit into small pieces. Add to the jelly. Pour into ice tray without separators. Keep it in the freezer till it sets.

Cut the jelly into rectangular pieces. Mix with cream and serve.

CUSTARD WITH NUTS

Serves 4-6

Preparation Time 30 Minutes

Ingredients :

½ litre milk

3 tbsp. custard powder

3 tbsp. sugar

20 almonds

20 cashewnuts

4 tbsp. kishmish

20 pistachios

4-5 green cardamoms

Method :

Make custard as given in the recipe of Fruit Custard with Jelly.

Add kishmish, crushed cardamom seeds and chopped nuts. Mix well. Cool in the fridge for one hour before serving.

It can be served luke warm also.

MANGO ICE CREAM

Serves 4-6
Preparation Time 4 Hours

Ingredients :

1 litre thick milk   2 large ripe mangoes
¾ cup sugar

Method :

Boil the milk till it evaporates to one-fourth in volume. Add sugar. Let it cool down.

Peel and cut the mangoes. Mix in an electric mixer. Add the thick milk and churn again till it becomes fluffy.

Freeze the mixture for 3-4 hours in freezer in a covered container.

Cut into pieces and serve.

KULFI

Serves 4-6
Preparation Time 8 Hours

Ingredients :

1 litre milk

1 cup sugar

1 tbsp. cornflour

1 cup falooda

1 cup chopped mixed nuts

4-5 green cardamoms

¼ tsp. kesar

Method :

Boil the milk till it reduces to one third in volume. Mix cornflour in 2 tbsp. of water and pour into milk. Cook stirring continuously for 5 minutes. Add sugar and cool.

Add nuts, crushed cardamom seeds and kesar. Mix well.

Pour it in into 4-6 large kulfi moulds and keep in the freezer for 6-8 hour.

Remove from the moulds and serve with falooda.

Chapter - IX
Tea Time
Snacks

CHAT PAPDI

Serves 4-6
Preparation Time 30 Minutes

Ingredients :

1 cup maida
1 tbsp. oil for the dough
Oil for frying
2 large potatoes
2 cups thick curd
1 cup saunth
(made from imli)

Salt to taste
1 tsp. jeera powder
1 tsp. chilli powder
1 tsp. kala namak
½ tsp. pepper

Method :

Sieve the maida. Make a stiff dough adding 1 tbsp. oil, a pinch of salt and water.

Divide the dough into 2 or 3 portions. Roll them out into very thin chapatis with the help of dry flour. Cut squares of 3-4 cm. or small rounds from these chapatis.

Heat oil. Fry few papdis at one time on very low heat till golden brown. let them cool down.

To make chat, boil, peel and cut the potatoes into small cubes. Beat the curd. Add all the masalas.

Arrange the papdis in a shallow dish. Put potato pieces over them. Pour curd and saunth. Sprinkle a little jeera and serve immediately.

PALAK CUTLETS

Serves 4-6
Preparation Time 30 Minutes

Ingredients :

250 gm. palak
1 large onion
1 large potato
1 tbsp. shelled peas
8 cloves of garlic
1 cm. piece ginger
2 tbsp. peanuts

2 tbsp. besan
½ tsp. chilli powder
½ tsp. garam masala
½ tsp. dhania powder
Salt to taste
Oil for frying
2-3 green chillis

Method :

Wash and cut palak very fine. Chop onion and potatoes. Grind garlic, green chilli and ginger into a fine paste. Mix all the vegetables with besan and masalas. Add a little water to make a smooth dough.

Make small balls and flatten them. Heat oil in a karahi. Fry 4-5 cutlets at a time till golden brown in colour.

Serve hot with tomato ketchup or pudina chutney.

ARBI CUTLETS

Serves 4-6
Preparation Time 30 Minutes

Ingredients :

½ kg. arbi	½ tsp. chilli powder
2 tbsp. peanuts .	½ tsp. amchur
2 tbsp. besan	½ tsp. garam masala
1 bunch coriander leaves	Salt to taste
2 green chillis	Oil for frying
½ tsp. ajwain	
2 tbsp. kishmish	

Method :

Boil arbi till tender. Peel and mash. Add coarsely ground, peanuts, besan, chopped green chillis, coriander leaves, kishmish and all the masalas. Mix well.

Make into round balls, flatten them or make any shape you like.

Heat oil in a karahi. Fry 4-5 cutlets at a time till golden brown.

Serve hot with podina chutney.

BREAD BALLS

Serves 4-6
Preparation Time 30 Minutes

Ingredients :

8 slices of bread
4 large potatoes
1 large onion
1 bunch coriander leaves
2 green chillis

½ tsp. chilli powder
1 tsp. coriander seeds
½ tsp. amchur
½ tsp. garam masala
Salt to taste
Oil for frying

Method :

Boil, peel and mash the potatoes. Chop onion, coriander leaves and green chillis. Mix with mashed potatoes and put all the masalas. Keep aside and let it cool down.

Soak one slice of bread in water at a time. Press with palm and remove the water. Put 1 tbsp. of potato mixture in the middle of bread and roll it into a ball. Make all the balls and keep aside for at least 10 minutes.

Heat oil in a karahi. Fry 3-4 balls at a time till golden brown in colour.

Serve hot with podina chutney and tomato ketchup.

ALU TIKKIES

Serves 4-6
Preparation Time 30 Minutes

Ingredients :

½ kg. potatoes
2 tbsp. channa dal
1 bunch coriander leaves
2 green chillis
1 cm. piece ginger
Salt to taste

2 cups thick curd
½ cup saunth
½ tsp. chilli powder
½ tsp. garam masala
Oil for frying

Method :

Boil, peel and mash the potatoes. Add a little salt and keep aside.

Wash and boil the channa dal till tender. Mash and mix with chopped coriander leaves, green chillis, ginger and all the masalas.

Take lemon size ball from the potato dough. Flatten it and put ½ tsp. of dal mixture on it. Roll it again into a ball and flatten it. Make all the tikkies and keep aside.

Heat a tawa. Put a little oil and arrange 6-7 tikkies on it. Pour some oil around them. Turn then over when brown on one side. Fry all the tikkies till golden brown and crisp on both the sides.

Serve with well beaten curd and saunth while the tikkies are hot.

SAMOSAS

Serves 4-6
Preparation Time 50 Minutes

Ingredients :

2 cups maida
6 large potatoes
4 green chillis
1 bunch coriander leaves
2 tbsp. oil for dough
Oil for frying

Salt to taste
½ tsp. chilli powder
1 tsp. dhanaia powder
1 tsp. amchur
½ tsp. ground pepper
1 tsp. jeera powder
1 tsp. coriander seeds

Method :

Boil, peel and break the potatoes into small pieces. Chop the coriander leaves and green chillis. Add coriander leaves and green chillis to the potatoes. Heat 1 tsp. oil. Put jeera, coriander seeds and coriander powder. Fry for a minute. Add this to the potato mixture. Mix well and keep aside.

Sieve the flour. Add a little salt and 2 tbsp. oil. Make a stiff dough with water. Make large lemon sized balls from it. Roll the balls one by one into thin, round chappatis. Cut into halves. Hold one portion in your hand. Place a little potato mixture on one half of the portion. Now fold over the another half portion over it sealing the edges with water.

Heat oil in a karahi. Fry 5-6 samosas at a time on medium heat tillgolden brown in colour. Serve hot with pudina or imli chutney.

KHASTAS

Serves 4-6
Preparation Time 50 Minutes

Ingredients :

2 cups maida

2 tbsp. oil for the dough

1 cup besan

Salt to taste

A pinch of hing

½ tsp. chilli powder

½ tsp. jeera powder

1 tsp. coriander powder

½ tsp. amchur

Oil for frying

Method :

Make a stiff dough of maida with 2 tbsp. oil and a pinch of salt. Knead it well.

Heat 1 tsp. oil in a frying pan. Roast besan in it on a very low heat till golden brown. Add all the masalas. Let it cool down.

Make small balls from the dough. Roll a little. Put 1 tsp. of besan and make it into ball again. Roll into thick puri.

Heat oil in karahi. Fry 5-6 khastas at a time on very low heat till light brown in colour.

Serve with podina or imli chutney.

These can be stored for 10-15 days.

PAKORAS

Serves 4-6

Preparation Time 30 Minutes

Ingredients :

2 cups besan
4 large potatoes
Salt to taste
Oil for frying

1 tsp. chilli powder
1 tsp. dhania powder
¼ tsp. ajwain

Method :

Sieve the besan. Add all the masalas and salt. Make a batter of medium consistency by adding water. Beat well and keep aside for about 15 minutes.

Peel, wash and cut the potatoes into thin round slices.

Heat oil in a karahi. Cover slices of potatoes with besan and drop in the oil one by one. Fry 7-8 pakoras at a time till golden brown.

Serve hot with podina chutney or tomato ketchup.

Pakoras can be made of other vegetables also like cauliflower, brinjals, onions, palak, marrow, green chillies, paneer etc.

BREAD UPMA

Serves 4-6
Preparation Time 20 Minutes

Ingredients :

6 slices of bread
1 large potato
1 large onion
1 large tomato
2 tbsp. shelled peas
2 tbsp. peanuts
4 green chillis
2 red chillis (dried)

1 bunch curry leaves
2 tsp. grated fresh coconut
1 tsp. mustard seeds
½ tsp. chilli powder
Salt to taste
1 tbsp. oil

Method :

Cut all the vegetables into small pieces.

Heat oil. Add mustard seeds, whole red chillies and curry leaves. Put potatoes and fry till light brown in colour. Add onions, shelled peas, peanuts, tomatoes and all the masalas. Cook for five minutes.

Sprinkle water over the slices of bread. Mash into fine pieces and add to the above mixture. Cook uncovered for 2-3 minutes stirring continuously.

Decorate with coconut and green chillis.

Serve hot with tomato ketchup.

SUJI UPMA

Serves 4-6
Preparation Time 20 Minutes

Ingredients :

2 cups suji	1 bunch curry leaves
2 tbsp. shelled peas	4 green chillis
2 tbsp. peanuts	4 red chillis whole
1 tbsp. channa and urd	½ tsp. chilli powder
dal each	1 tsp. mustard seeds
2 tbsp. grated fresh	Salt to taste
coconut	1 tbsp. oil

Method :

Cut the green chillis into small pieces.

Heat oil. Add whole red chillis, mustard seeds and dals. Now add peanuts, peas, green chillis and curry leaves. Cook for 2-3 minutes. Add 4 cups of water, salt and chilli powder. When water starts boiling, put suji. Lower the heat and cook stirring continuously till all water dries up. Remove from heat and leave it covered for ten minutes.

Decorate with grated coconut and serve with tomato ketchup.

VEGETARIAN KABABS

Serves 4-6
Preparation Time 50 Minutes

Ingredients :

2 cups kaley channay	Salt to taste
2 cm. piece ginger	½ tsp. chilli powder
10 cloves of garlic	1 tsp. dhania (whole)
4 green chillis	½ tsp. amchur
1 big pinch of hing	Oil for frying

Method :

Wash and soak the channa overnight. Grind it coarsely with a little water along with ginger, garlic and green chillis. Add all the masalas and mix well.

Make small balls out of this dough and flatten them.

Heat a tawa. Smear oil over it. Put 4-5 kababs at a time. Cook on low heat pouring a little oil over them till brown on one side. Turn them and fry the other side also.

Serve hot with podina chutney and onion rings.

DHOKLA

Serves 4-6

Preparation Time 30 Minutes

Ingredients :

1½ cups besan

½ cup rice

1 tsp. baking powder

½ cup sour curd

1 tbsp. oil

8 green chillis

½ tsp. chilli powder

A pinch of haldi

1 tsp. mustard seeds

1 tbsp. grated fresh coconut

Salt to taste

1 bunch curry leaves

Method :

Wash and soak the rice in water for about half an hour. Grind it into fine paste. Mix besan, rice paste, salt, haldi, chilli powder and curd to make a batter of medium consistency. Add a little water if necessary. Mix baking powder with 2 tsp. of water and add to the mixture. Beat well.

Grease a round mould. Pour the above mixture into mould and steam bake in pressure cooker for about 15 minutes in it. Don't put the pressure weight. To test insert a needle in it. If it comes out clean, dhokla is ready. If mixture sticks, cook for another 5 minutes. Cool for 5 minutes and cut into square pieces.

Heat oil in frying pan. Add mustard seeds, curry leaves and green chillis. Pour this over dhokla. Garnish with grated coconut.

POTATO CUTLETS

Serves 4-6
Preparation Time 30 Minutes

Ingredients :

½ kg. potatoes
2 tbsp. shelled peas
1 small onion
1 bunch coriander leaves
3 slices of bread

½ tsp. chilli powder
½ tsp. garam masala
Salt to taste
Oil for frying

Method :

Boil, peel and mash the potatoes. Soak bread in water for half a minute. Press it to remove water. Mix with potatoes, shelled peas, chopped onions, coriander leaves and all the masalas.

Make small balls from the prepared mixture. Keep them round or flatten them.

Heat oil in a frying pan. When the ghee is smoking hot, put 4-5 cutlets at a time and fry till golden brown. Serve hot with tomato ketchup.

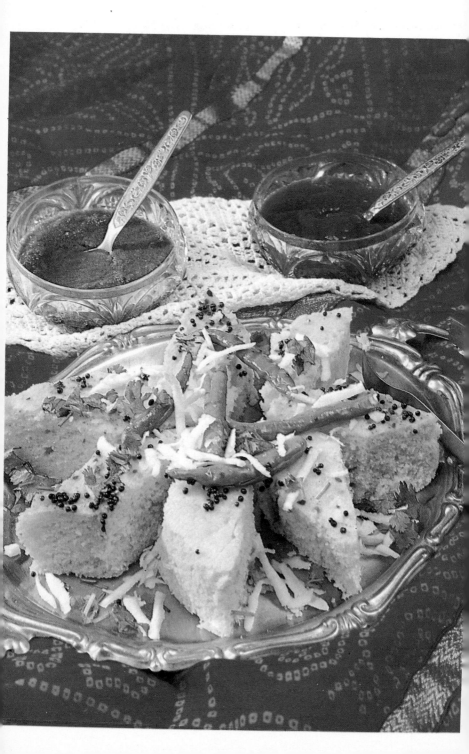

GOLGAPPAS

Serves 4-6
Preparation Time 30 Minutes

Ingredients :

1 cup maida	50 gm. tamarind
2 tbsp. suji	1 cup sugar
2 large boiled potatoes	1 tsp. chilli powder
1 cup boiled kabli	1 tsp. kala namak
channas	1 tsp. jeera powder
Oil for frying	1 tsp. pepper
1 bunch podina	2 large lemons
2 tsp. salt	

Method :

Make a stiff dough of maida and suji with water. Take very little dough and roll golgappas of 3 to 4 cm. diametre size. Keep them on a damp cloth.

Heat oil and fry these golgappas 5-6 at a time. They should rise like balloons. Fry on low heat till golden brown in colour.

Soak tamarind in one cup of water for about one hour. Extract the juice. Add one jug of water, juice of lemons, sugar, salt and all the masalas. Add paste of podina also. Cool this jaljeera in the refrigerator.

Peel and mash the potatoes. Mix with channas. Add

a little salt and pepper.

To serve golgappas, make a small hole in each golgappa. Put a little potato and channa mixture in it. Fill with jaljeera and serve immediately.

MATHRIS

Serves 4-6
Preparation Time 40 Minutes

Ingredients :

2 cups maida   Salt to taste
4 tbsp. oil for the dough ½ tsp. ajwain
Oil for frying

Method :

Sieve the maida. Add salt ajwain, 4 tbsp. oil and a little water to make a stiff dough. Knead it well.

Make lemon size balls from the dough. Roll them into thick round mathris.

Heat oil. Fry 5-6 mathris at a time on very low heat till they are golden brown in colour and are well cooked.

Another method is to roll the dough into a thin chapati and cut it into small squares or rounds and fry in the oil.

When cool keep them into an air-tight container. These can be stored for 2-3 weeks.

BESAN SEV

Serves 4-6
Preparation Time 30 Minutes

Ingredients :

1 cup besan

1 tbsp. oil for dough

Oil for frying

Salt to taste

¼ tsp. chilli powder

¼ tsp. haldi powder

Method :

Sieve besan. Add oil, salt, chilli powder and haldi. Make a stiff dough with water. Knead it well.

Heat oil in a karahi. Put a little dough into sevia making machine. Press it over the hot oil. It will come out in the form of thin sevia. Fry till light brown in colour.

Cool the sev and store in an air-tight container.

CHAKLI

Serves 4-6
Preparation Time 30 Minutes

Ingredients :

2 cups rice flour   1 tsp. dry coriander
½ cup besan   (whole)
3 tbsp. oil for the dough ½ tsp. chilli powder
Oil for frying   1 tbsp. til seeds
A pinch of hing   Salt to taste

Method :

Sieve the besan and rice flour. Add oil, salt, chilli powder, til seeds and dhania. Make a stiff dough with water. Knead it well.

Put a little dough into chakli maker. Press it and make round chaklis (like jalebis). Keep in a tray. Heat oil in a karahi. Fry 5-6 chaklis at a time on medium heat till golden brown.

Cool them and store in an air-tight container.

POTATO WAFERS

Serves 4-6
Preparation Time 20 Minutes

Ingredients :

8 large potatoes   Salt to taste
Oil for frying

Method :

Peel and wash the potatoes. Cut them into very thin round slices. Keep these in salted water for about half an hour. Dry them over a clean kitchen towel.

Heat oil. Fry handful of wafers at a time on medium heat till crisp and light brown in colour.

Serve when cooled.

You can store these in air tight containers for 2-3 weeks.

FINGER CHIPS

Serves 4-6
Preparation Time 20 Minutes

Ingredients :

8 large potatoes	Salt to taste
Oil for frying	1 tsp. pepper

Method :

Peel, wash and dry the potatoes. Cut into 1 cm. square, long strips.

Heat oil. Fry handful of potato pieces at a time on medium heat till golden brown in colour and soft. Sprinkle with salt and pepper.

Serve hot with tomato ketchup.

RICE KACHRIS

Serves 4-6
Preparation Time 30 Minutes

Ingredients :

1 cup rice   ½ tsp. jeera
4 cups water   1 tsp. salt

Method :

Wash and soak the rice in four cups of water overnight.

Cook in the pressure cooker for 2 minutes after the whistling starts. Let it cool down. Mash it well with a spoon. Add salt and jeera.

Spread a polyethylene sheet on a table. Take a little portion of above mixture at a time and pass it through a chakli machine making round chaklis. Keep in the sun till these dry up completely.

Store these in a tin. Fry in hot oil before serving.

GULGULAS

Serves 4-6
Preparation Time 20 Minutes

Ingredients :

1 cup moong dal
(with husk)
1 large onion
4 green chillis
1 bunch of coriander
leaves
2 tbsp. grated paneer

Salt to taste
½ tsp. chilli powder
½ tsp. whole dhania
A pinch of hing
Oil for frying

Method :

Soak the dal for 3-4 hours. Remove the husk. Grind the dal into a coarse paste. Cut onion, green chillis and coriander leaves into small pieces. Mix all these ingredients, paneer, masalas and dal. Beat the mixture with hand for five minutes.

Heat oil in a karahi. Make small balls of dal and fry on medium heat till golden brown in colour.

Serve hot with podina chutney.

FRUIT CHAT

Serves 4-6
Preparation Time 20 Minutes

Ingredients :

2 apples
2 oranges
4 bananas
1 large potato (boiled)
1 large tomato
2 kheeras
½ tsp. kala namak

Salt to taste
½ tsp. chilli powder
½ tsp. jeera powder
½ tsp. pepper powder
1 lemon
1 tbsp. sugar

Method :

Cut all the fruit, potato, tomato and kheera into small pieces.

Mix with all the masalas, sugar, salt and lemon juice. Mix well and cool in refrigerator before serving.

It is better if you cool all the fruit before cutting and then mix with masala and serve immediately.

KABULI CHANNA CHAT

Serves 4-6
Preparation Time 30 Minutes

Ingredients :

2 cups kabuli channa	Salt to taste
2 large potatoes	½ tsp. chilli powder
1 large onion	½ tsp. jeera powder
1 large tomato	½ tsp. pepper
4 green chillis	½ tsp. kala namak
1 lemon	1 bunch dhania leaves

Method :

Wash and soak the channa for about 5 hours. Boil in pressure cooker for 20 minutes till tender. Boil and cut the potatoes into small cubes. Cut onion, tomato, green chillis and dhania into very small pieces.

Mix channa, all the vegetables and masalas. Pour juice of the lemon and mix well. Keep in refrigerator before serving.

Instead of kabuli channas you can use green peas also.

SPROUTED MOONG CHAT

Serves 4-6
Preparation Time 15 Minutes

Ingredients :

1 cup moong (whole)	Salt to taste
1 large potato	½ tsp. chilli powder
1 large onion	½ tsp. pepper
1 large tomato	½ tsp. kala namak
4 green chillis	½ tsp. jeera powder
1 lemon	1 bunch dhania (green)
1 kheera	

Method :

Wash and soak the moong overnight. Remove water and put the soaked moong in a shallow container. Cover it and leave for 24 hours in winters and 10-12 hours in summers to sprout.

Boil and cut the potato in very small pieces. Cut onion, tomato, kheera, dhania and green chillis also into small pieces. Mix the vegetables, moong sprouts and all the masalas. Sprinkle juice of the lemon. Cool it and serve.

Chapter - X
Chutneys, Pickles And Jams

PODINA OR DHANIA CHUTNEY

Preparation Time 20 Minutes

Ingredients :

1 bunch podina or	½ tsp. red chillis
coriander leaves	Salt to taste
4 green chillies	1 large lemon or 2 tsp.
1 cm. piece ginger	amchur or anardana
1 large onion	1 tsp. sugar
8 cloves of garlic	

Method :

Take the leaves and tender stems of podina or dhania. Wash them thoroughly. Peel and chop ginger, garlic and onion. Chop green chillis also.

Grind the above ingredients to a fine paste. Add lemon juice, salt, chilli powder and sugar. Mix well.

This chutney can be stored for a week or even more in the fridge.

PEANUT CHUTNEY

Preparation Time 20 Minutes

Ingredients :

½ cup peanut

2 tbsp. channa dal

2 tbsp. urd dal

2 tbsp. grated coconut

6 green chillis

1 tsp. chilli powder

Salt to taste

1 large lemon or

2 tbsp. sour curd

1 tsp. mustard seeds

1 tsp. oil

Method :

Soak the peanuts in water for half an hour. Roast the dals on tawa.

Grind dals, peanuts, coconut and green chillies to a fine paste. Add salt, chilli powder and lemon juice to it. Mix well.

Heat oil. Put mustard seeds in it. Pour it over the chutney.

IMLI CHUTNEY OR SAUNTH

Preparation Time 20 Minutes

Ingredients :

50 gm. tamarind
100 gm. gur or 1 cup sugar
1 tbsp. kishmish
4 dried dates
1 ripe banana (optional)
1 tsp. dry ginger powder

½ tsp. chilli powder
1 tsp. jeera powder
½ tsp. kala namak
1 tsp. garam masala
Salt to taste

Method :

Boil gur and tamarind with half a cup of water for about 10 minutes. Take out the pulp through a strainer.

Add all the masalas and mix well. Boil for 2-3 minutes.

Chop the dates and cut banana into small pieces. Clean and wash the kishmish. Add this to the saunth and mix well.

Saunth can be stored for a fortnight or so in the fridge.

TOMATO CHUTNEY

Preparation Time 60 Minutes

Ingredients :

1 kg. tomatoes
400 gm. sugar
2 tbsp. kishmish
4 dried dates

1 tsp. red chillis
1 tsp. garam masala
1 tsp. salt
2 tbsp. vinegar or juice
of one lemon

Method :

Wash and cut the tomatoes into small pieces. Add sugar and bring it to boil. Reduce the heat and cook it on medium heat for about 20 minutes. Add all the masalas, kishmish, chopped dates and vinegar. Cook for another 15 minutes till it is thick and is of medium consistency.

Let it cool completely.

Store in a dry bottle.

MANGO CHUTNEY — NO. 1

Preparation Time 60 Minutes

Ingredients :

1 kg. mangoes (raw)   2 tsp. salt
750 gm. sugar   2 tsp. garam masala
2 tbsp. kishmish   1 tsp. red chillis
4 dried dates   ½ cup vinegar
2 cm. piece ginger

Method :

Wash and dry the mangoes with a towel. Peel and grate them. Cut the ginger and dates into thin, long slices.

Mix all the ingredients except vinegar. Boil for about half an hour. Reduce the heat and cook for another ten minutes. Add vinegar and cook stirring continuously till it thickens.

Let it cool down. Wash and dry the bottles properly. Fill the chutney into bottles.

MANGO CHUTNEY — NO. 2

Preparation Time 30 Minutes

Ingredients :

1 kg. mangoes (raw)	1 tsp. salt
750 gm sugar	1 tsp. kala namak
2 tbsp. kishmish	2 tsp. garam masala
4 dried dates	1 tsp. red chillis

Method :

Wash, dry, peel and grate the mangoes. Cut the dates into thin, long slices. Clean the kishmish.

Take a stainless steel saucepan. Put the grated mangoes at the bottom then all the masalas, kishmish and dates. Cover this with sugar.

Keep it in the sun covering the saucepan with a thin muslin cloth. Stir the mixture next day. Keep it in the sun for 15 days stirring it daily.

Fill it in well washed and dried bottles.

MANGO PICKLE (WITH OIL)

Preparation Time 40 Minutes

Ingredients :

1 kg. green raw mangoes   50 gm. chilli powder
400 ml. mustard oil   50 gm. saunf
150 gm. salt   50 gm. methi seeds
25 gm. turmeric powder   25 gm. onion seeds
  (kalaunji)

Method :

Wash and clean the mangoes. Dry them with a clean towel. Cut the mangoes into 8 pieces each lengthwise or into smaller pieces.

Put 4 tbsp. oil in all the masalas. Mix well. Mix this masala with mango pieces. Put this into clean glass jar and keep it in the sun for two days shaking 3-4 times a day.

On the third day pour the oil over it and keep it in the sun for a week or so. This pickle should be completely covered with oil.

MANGO PICKLE (WITHOUT OIL)

Preparation Time 30 Minutes

Ingredients :

1 kg. green raw mangoes   10 gm. asafoetida
100 gm. chilli powder   150 gm. salt

Method :

Wash, dry and peel the mangoes. Cut them into small pieces.

Mix these pieces with salt, chilli powder and asafoetida. Put it in a glass jar and keep it in the sun for 7-8 days shaking 3-4 times a day.

CAULIFLOWER, CARROT & TURNIP PICKLE (SWEET)

Preparation Time 40 Minutes

Ingredients :

½ kg. carrots
½ kg. turnip
1 small cauliflower
2½ tbsp. salt
4 tbsp. mustard oil
1 tbsp. chilli powder
1 tbsp. turmeric powder

2 tbsp. mustard seeds powder
2 cm. piece ginger
10 cloves of garlic
25 gm. tamarind
150 gm. gur or
½ cup sugar
½ cup vinegar

Method :

Prepare the vegetables as in the previous recipe.

Mince garlic and ginger. Soak tamarind in a little water and extract pulp.

Heat oil in a pan. Put ginger, garlic and crushed gur. Cook for 2-3 minutes. Add tamarind pulp, vinegar and all the masalas. Cook for 3-4 minutes. Remove from heat.

Put all the vegetables in the above mixture. Mix well and let it cool. Put it in a glass jar and keep in the sun for 5-6 days shaking daily.

CAULIFLOWER, CARROT & TURNIP PICKLE

Preparation Time 30 Minutes

Ingredients :

½ kg. turnip
½ kg. carrots
1 small cauliflower
2 tbsp. salt

1 tbsp. chilli powder
1 tbsp. turmeric powder
2 tbsp. mustard seeds powder
3 tbsp. mustard oil

Method :

Wash the vegetables. Cut carrots into small pieces length wise. Cut thin round slices of turnip. Break the cauliflower into small pieces.

Boil water in a big pan. When water starts boiling, put all the vegetables in it. Keep the vegetables in water for 2 minutes. Take out the vegetables from the water. Dry them on a clean towel for 3-4 hours in the sun.

Mix all the masalas and oil with vegetables thoroughly. Put it in a glass jar. Keep it in the sun for 4-5 days shaking 2-3 times a day.

STUFFED CHILLIS PICKLE

Preparation Time 40 Minutes

Ingredients :

½ kg. fresh red chillis
or thick green chillis
3 tbsp. saunf
2 tbsp. methi seeds
3 tbsp. mustard seeds
2 tbsp. amchur

1 tbsp. chilli powder
½ cup mustard oil
3 tbsp. salt
2 tbsp. dhania powder

Method :

Clean the saunf, methi seeds and mustard seeds. Dry grind these to powder.

Wash and dry the chillis. Cut them from the top and take out the seeds.

Mix all the masalas and seeds from the chillis with half the mustard oil. Fill this masala in the chillis. Put these chillis in a clean, dry glass jar. Pour the remaining oil and masalas over them. Keep in the sun for 5-6 days shaking them daily.

LEMON PICKLE (NO. 1).

Preparation Time 30 Minutes

Ingredients :

1 kg. lemons (slightly yellow in colour)

2 tbsp. garam masala

250 gm. sugar

2 tbsp. ajwain

5 tbsp. salt

1 tbsp. chilli powder

2 tbsp kala namak

Method :

Wash and dry the lemons with a towel. Extract juice from half of the lemons. Slit the remaining lemons into four.

Mix all the masalas and sugar. Fill the masala in the lemons. Keep all the lemons in a glass jar. Pour the lemon juice over them. Put the left over masala in it. Shake well. Keep it in the sun for 20-25 days shaking daily.

The pickle is ready when the skin turns brown in colour.

LEMON PICKLE (NO. 2)

Preparation Time 30 Minutes

Ingredients :

½ kg. lemons   4 tbsp. salt
250 gm. green chillies   2 tsp. pepper
250 gm. ginger

Method :

Wash and dry the lemons. Peel ginger, wash it and dry. Cut the chillis into small pieces. Cut the ginger into long, thick slices. Cut the lemons into 8 pieces each leaving 4 lemons for juice.

Take out the juice of 4 lemons. Put the lemon pieces, ginger and green chillis in a clean, dry glass jar. Put salt, pepper and juice of the lemons.

Mix well and keep in the sun for 2-3 days. The pickle is ready in 2-3 days.

RASBERRY JAM

Preparation Time 60 Minutes

Ingredients :

1 kg. ripe raspberries
750 gm. sugar

4 drops of yellow colour
(edible)
1 lemon

Method :

Wash and cut the raspberries into two pieces each. Keep in a thick bottomed pan and cook on a medium heat for about 20 minutes. Add sugar and cook for another half an hour strring occasionally until thick. Add the lemon juice and yellow colour and boil for another 5 minutes. Remove from heat.

Clean and dry the bottles. Fill the jam when it is cool.

To test whether jam is ready or not, take water in a cup. Pour a few drops of hot jam in it. If it does not dissolve in water and settles at the bottom, it is ready. If it dissolves in water, boil for another few minutes and test again.

MIXED FRUIT JAM

Preparation Time 60 Minutes

Ingredients :

½ kg. ripe pineapple   1¼ kg. sugar
½ kg. apples   5 drops of red colour
½ kg. pears   (edible)
½ kg. plums   1 lemon

Method :

Wash, peel and cut the fruit into small pieces.

Keep in a thick bottomed pan and cook for 20 minutes on medium heat. Don't put any water. Add the sugar, colour and juice of the lemon and cook for another half an hour or more until thick.

Test it by the water test as in the previous recipe. Let it cool down and fill it in clean, dry and air-tight bottles.

MANGO JAM

Preparation Time 60 Minutes

Ingredients :

1 kg. raw mangoes   A pinch of yellow colour.
700 gm. sugar   (edible)

Method :

Wash and boil the mangoes for about 20 minutes or till they are tender. Remove from water.

Take out the pulp from the mangoes. Mix with sugar and yellow colour. Keep in a thick bottomed pan and boil them till it thickens.

Do the water test. Keep it in clean, dry and air-tight bottles.

GUAVA JELLY

Preparation Time 60 minutes

Ingredients :

1 kg guavas (ripe)   2 lemons
600 gm sugar   ½ litre. water

Method :

Wash and cut the guavas into small pieces.

Keep the guavas and water in a thick bottomed pan. Boil for about half an hour on a medium heat till the guavas are very tender. Strain through a muslin cloth and collect the juice in the pan. Hang the cloth with guava pulp on a nail or press with very heavy stone so that the juice comes out in the pan. It will take about 5-6 hours to extract the juice.

Now mix the sugar with juice and boil on high heat. When it reduces to half, add the lemon juice and keep on boiling till thick.

Do the same water test as in the previous recipe. Let it cool down and fill in dry, clean and air-tight bottles.

GLOSSARY OF INDIAN TERMS

Aam	-	Mango
Atta	-	Whole wheat flour
Alu	-	Potato
Adrak	-	Ginger
Ajwain	-	Parsley seeds
Amchur	-	Dried mango powder
Anardana	-	Dried pomegranate seeds
Arbi	-	Calocasia
Baigan	-	Brinjal, Aubergine
Besan	-	Gram flour
Bhindi	-	Lady's fingers
Badam	-	Almond
Band Gobi	-	Cabbage
Boondi	-	Fried savoury drops of gram flour
Besan Sev	-	Fried savoury long strips of gram flour
Bhallas	-	Fried flat balls of lentil flour
Channa Dal	-	Gram dal
Chakli	-	Savoury long strips of gram flour and rice flour
Dal	-	Pulses or lentils
Dahi	-	Curd

Dhania	-	Coriander
Dhokla	-	Savoury steam baked cubes of gram flour and rice flour
Elaichi	-	Cardamom
Falooda	-	Freshly made vermicillis of cornflour
Garam masala	-	Mixture of powdered peppercorn, cloves, cinnamon, black cardamom, cummin seed and bay leaves.
Ghee	-	Clarified butter
Gur	-	Jaggery
Golgappa	-	Fried small round hollow wafer of flour
Haldi	-	Turmeric
Hing	-	Asafoetida
Imli	-	Tamarind
Idli maker	-	Perforated container used for steam baking
Jeera	-	Cummin seeds
Kathal	-	Jackfruit
Kishmish	-	Raisins
Kalaunji	-	Onion seeds
Karahi	-	Deep frying pan
Kala channa	-	Horse gram

Kala namak	-	Rock salt
Kabuli channa	-	White gram
Kofta	-	Fried round balls of vegetables
Kashiphal	-	Pumpkin
Kamal Kakri	-	Lotus stem
Kheera	-	Cucumber
Karela	-	Bitter gourd
Kesar	-	Saffron
Khoya	-	Fresh milk evaporated till it solidifies
Lauki	-	Marrow
Maida	-	Refined wheat flour
Methi	-	Fenugreek
Masala	-	spices
Moong	-	Green gram
Mooli	-	Radish
Mattar	-	Fresh green peas
Mathris	-	Savoury fried rounds or strips of flour
Makhaney	-	Lotus fruit
Palak	-	Spinach
Petha	-	Red pumpkin
Paneer	-	Cottage cheese

Podina	-	Mint
Pista	-	Pistachios
Puri	-	Indian fried bread
Phool Gobi	-	Cauliflower
Pakori	-	Fried balls of green gram
Papdi	-	Fried small round wafers of flour
Rajma	-	Red beans
Raie	-	Mustard seeds
Rooh Afza Sharbat	-	Rose syrup
Rasgulla	-	Round balls of cottage cheese in sugar syrup
Rasmalai	-	Round flattered balls of cottage cheese in sweetened condensed or evaporated milk
Saunf	-	Aniseed
Shalgam	-	Turnip
Sarson	-	Fresh green mustard leaves
Sabut	-	Whole
Sevia	-	Vermicilli
Samber Powder	-	Mixture of powdered red chillies, cummin seed, coriander seeds, asafoetida, fenugreek, mustard seeds and dried curry leaves

Suji	-	Samolina
Saunth	-	Imli chutney (Recipe given)
Til	-	Sesame
Tawa	-	Flat round iron plate for making Indian bread
Thali	-	Plate with a little raised edges
Urd	-	Black gram
Upma	-	Savoury dish of samolina & mixed vegetables
Tbsp.	-	Table spoon
Tsp.	-	Tea spoon

GLOSSARY OF ENGLISH TERMS

Almonds	-	Badam
Aniseed	-	Saunf
Apple	-	Seb
Banana	-	Kela
Beet root	-	Chukander
Bread	-	Pav roti
Brinjal	-	Baigan
Carrot	-	Gajar
Cinnamon	-	Dalchini
Chilli	-	Mirch
Clove	-	Lawang
Cashewnuts	-	Kaju
Coconut	-	Narial
Coriander	-	Dhania
Cucumber	-	Kheera
Curd	-	Dahi
Cauliflower	-	Phul Gobi
Cabbage	-	Bund Gobi
Capsicum	-	Simlamirch
Flour	-	Maida
Garlic	-	Lahsun

Groundnut/Peanuts	-	Moongphali
Ginger	-	Adrak
Gram flour	-	Besan
Guava	-	Amrud
Lemon	-	Nimbu
Lady's fingers	-	Bhindi
Mint	-	Podina
Mustard seeds	-	Raie / Sarson dana
Pepper	-	Kali mirch
Pineapple	-	Annanas
Pumpkin	-	Kashiphal - Kaddu
Sieve	-	Chanani
Spinach	-	Palak
Tomatoes	-	Tamater
Tamarind	-	Imli
Turmeric	-	Haldi
Turnip	-	Shalgam
Walnut	-	Akhrot